2014 State of
Participatory Democracy
Report

The Hunger Project, in partnership with the UN Democracy Fund

Contact info@thp.org for permission to reprint.

The Hunger Project
5 Union Square West
New York, NY 10003
Telephone: +1-212-251-9100
www.thp.org
Project site: localdemocracy.net

Photo credits: The Hunger Project

Good News for Democracy

Yes, it's true. While the world stands shocked at despotic acts of brutality in armed conflicts for political domination, there is another story that goes largely unreported: the daily progress of millions of women and men as they take charge of their lives and destinies at the local level.

The central lesson of this year's State of Participatory Democracy Report is that in many countries where national-level democracy and respect for human rights may be fragile, the roots of democratic values are being are being deepened and seeing new legislation. This expansion of participatory local democracy has yielded improvement of public services and inclusion of an active civil society in the formation of new laws.

This is not to say that the overall space for effective, transparent, accountable local governance is in good shape - far from it. However, what we do see in this year's report is more:

- **Decentralization:** Countries long seen as highly centralized have transferred more autonomy to local governments.
- **Investment in local capacity:** Countries that are desperately poor have made dramatic strides in health, agriculture and education by investing in training tens of thousands of teachers, extension agents and front-line health workers.
- **Women's leadership:** More countries are establishing quotas and seat reservations in government to ensure that women have a voice in the decisions affecting their lives.
- **Mechanisms for social accountability:** More women and men are gaining opportunities to hold local leaders accountable.
- **Enabling technologies:** From big corporations to the villages of Bangladesh, internet and computer technology is being applied to make information and public services more accessible, facilitate communications between citizens and their government, and increase transparency and accountability.
- **Collaboration between government and civil society:** While some governments are rrestricting civil society - particularly human rights and environment activists - other governments have established solid, formal and coordinated mechanisms to partner with civil society.
- **Clarity on what works:** The key factors measured in our multidimensional index are becoming better known and more broadly recognized, leading local governance activists to increase their call for a global charter on local governance.
- **More recognition at the global level:** As the global community has worked earnestly - in the most participatory policy dialogue the world has ever seen - to develop a set of Post-2015 Sustainable Development Goals, the critical importance of local governance is [at last] being recognized.

Expanding the Global Community of Practice

Our Global Community of Practice reached out to pioneering - and sometimes courageous - civil society organizations (CSOs) that have invested decades in shifting national policies towards greater citizen engagement and local democracy in areas where democracy is most fragile in Africa, the Middle East, the Balkans and Central Asia. This year, the Community also included participation from the MENA region (Middle East and North Africa), Arab countries and Western Asia.

We invited these CSOs to organize multi-stakeholder focus group discussions consisting of local and central government officials, civil society, women's groups, academia, the private sector and international agencies (where relevant). We asked each focus group to reach consensus answers for each survey question, and provided space for comments where this proved impossible.

The CSOs shared their reflections on the value of this multi-sectoral process for their own work. These reflections are available on our website: http://localdemocracy.net.

Improving the Quality of the Data

One major discovery last year was that virtually no individual practitioner has ready access to the information needed for assessing all dimensions of participatory local democracy, both in terms of what is established by law and the actual reality on the ground.

Last year, we divided the assessment process into two surveys: one for those knowledgeable about the law, and one for those knowledgeable about ground realities. Despite extra outreach effort this required, we were still dissatisfied with the quality of most resulting data. Of the 90 countries that submitted data, we concluded that it was was only sufficiently complete in 35 countries.

We determined that the best approach for 2014 was to (1) streamline the assessment into one survey instrument - addressing both legal and implementation with more objective questions - and (2) disseminate the assessment surveys to multi-stakeholder focus groups rather than individuals.

Organization of this report

In the following pages context includes:

- **Country profiles,** in alphabetical order, on the state of Participatory Local Democracy in 33 countries.
- **Seven "Profiles of Practice"** that highlight important aspects of the evolution of decentralization in Bolivia, Indonesia, Jordan, Lebanon, Malawi, Morocco and Senegal.
- **Text of the 2014 Survey**
- **Results and Rankings of the 2014 Survey,** which include data from the countries that held focus groups (in **bold**) and data submitted by individuals from an additional 20 countries (in *italics*).

Survey Dimensions in Brief

Active Citizenry
- **Aware:** citizens are knowledgeable about their rights and informed of government decisions
- **Inclusive:** women and other marginalized groups are guaranteed a voice in decision-making processes
- **Organized:** citizens are organized to collectively negotiate with local government
- **Participating:** citizens, civil society groups, and local private sector can lobby in local government structures

Political Decentralization
- **Democratic:** open elections are held for office at all levels of government
- **Transparent:** government actions, decisions and decision-making processes are open to an appropriate level of scrutiny by other parts of the government, citizens and, in some instances, outside institutions
- **Accountable:** mechanisms exist for citizens to intervene in the policy making process, and have means to redress instances of corruption
- **Autonomous:** local government has the power, capacity and flexibility to respond to social changes and demands, takes into account the expectations of civil society in identifying general public interest, and is willing to critically re-examine the role of government

Administrative Decentralization
- **Decentralized:** a representative government exists at a close and accessible level to the people and is responsible for service delivery; a transparent legal framework supports decentralization; all laws, codes and regulations are equally enforced by the government
- **Trained:** local government officials and civil society organizations supporting local government receive systemic and consistent training
- **Effective:** government strives to produce quality public outputs - such as cost-effective service delivery to systems - and ensures that they meet the original intentions of policy-makers

Fiscal Decentralization
- **Supported:** local government is able to mobilize local resources and receives a share (ideally 20+%) of public resources
- **Independent:** local government exercises freedom to allocate funds for locally-identified priorities

Multi-sectoral Planning
- **Capacity:** local government has the mandate, skills, and timely resources to engage stakeholders in long-term planning for basic services
- **Deliberative:** citizens participate in meaningful discussions about local priorities and their decisions are reflected in the governing process

Observations from the 2014 Data

- **Africa - the Surprise Winner:** Sub-Saharan Africa scored very highly - just behind the most developed countries. A subset of four African countries (Burundi, Senegal, Ethiopia, Liberia) are of the the top-five ranked. These "new" decentralizers scored significantly higher than Africa's older decentralizers - Uganda and Ghana - as well as all other countries. This shows that both strong commitment and implementation of decentralization. For example, **Ethiopia** - a large, federalized country - has made large-scale investments in community-driven development, training large numbers of health workers and agricultural extension workers at the local level. **The gap** between laws and implementation is quite large; the legal framework scores highest of all regions, while perceptions of implementation lag far behind.
- **MENA** (Middle East and North Africa): scored lowest, which is not surprising as most of these countries are not considered democratic republics even at the national level. Yet, as shown in the Profiles of Practice for Morocco and Jordan, there are new initiatives underway for decentralization in these countries.
- **Central and Western Asia:** these newly included nations scored surprisingly close to the middle and consistently across dimensions, with a fairly modest gap between laws and implementation.
- **East and Southern Asia:** Indonesia ranked highest in this group, despite showing the largest gap between recently established decentralization and respondents' perception of implementation. Indonesia has its own local governance index, which is featured in their Profile of Practice.
- **Latin America:** this group scored very high in its legal structure, but has the most severe **gap** between legal framework and people's perception of implementation - particularly in the fiscal and planning sectors.
- **Developed Countries:** most that participated this year scored best as a region, reflecting long-standing systems of local democracy, although not as strongly as some might expect. For example, the US national government is "newer" than its local governments and, due to such, does not have a national policy framework for the role of local governments.
- **Psychology:** although we have endeavored to make the legal and perceptual survey questions as objective as possible, we suspect that the wide variations in the gap between law and perceived reality may reflect a degree of "expectation" bias – that people's optimism or pessimism about the likelihood of near-term progress may influence their perceptions.

How should it work?

A wise saying goes: "all politics is local." It reflects the wisdom that those issues that really matter in people's daily life – water, sanitation, primary health care, primary education, year-round access to affordable and nutritious food, access to markets and employment opportunities, basic safety and social justice – must be resolved locally. This requires responsive, effective local governance.

A simple way to think about this issue is to ask this question: if things were really sustainably working here, how would they work? If I'm a citizen with rights (not a subject of an authority on whose favor or whims I depend) - how can I work with my fellow citizens to make my community sustainable?

Our multidimensional index goes beyond the traditional three dimensions of government decentralization (political, administrative and fiscal). It starts with an active citizenry, and includes the vital role of the social and private sector in planning processes.

So - imagine you are a mother, and your child's teacher is not regularly showing up to class. What do you do?

First - you should be empowered as an Active Citizen. You need to be aware of what you can do and how you can do it. Your country should have a Right to Information Law in place that allows you to find out - in a reasonable length of time - whether this is just your problem, or whether it is happening everywhere. Your local government should be providing oversight of the schools, and posting a "citizen charter" telling you who to contact for each public service. The process should be **inclusive**: officials should listen to you as they would a man, and there should be a woman in authority whom you can turn to. You should be **organized**, as a member of what is hopefully a regularly participatory parent and teacher association (PTA), which should give you strength and some access to key people. If necessary, your PTA should have the right to take the issue to the courts.

Second - you should have a government that represents your local interests. Your local council should have been **democratically elected,** not appointed or hereditary, and you should be able to run for office if you so desire. Your local council should be autonomous, responding to your interests rather than not merely following orders from above. Bureaucrats should not be able to remove or override the decisions of your local council without going to courts. Your local council should be honest, **accountable** (as demonstrated by audits and reports) and **transparent** in its actions.

Third - public services should be locally administered. The local council should be able to require that the teacher be fired, even if he is the nephew of the governor. To this end, local administrators should be **trained** and **effective** at doing their jobs.

Fourth - your local government should be well funded. Perhaps the teacher has not been paid in three months, because the central government failed to transfer money. Ideally, your community should be able to raise its own revenues, or - if too poor - receive central funds through a transparent mechanism. The local council should be **independent** in setting its own budgets and controlling its own funds. It should not have to wait for layers of bureaucracy to make approvals.

Fifth - your community should be able to plan. Perhaps the teacher is not coming to work because the roads are unsafe or there are no functioning toilets in the school. The previous local council had planned to fix it, but a the newly elected one discarded the old plans and has not created new ones. The community needs a **long-term plan** that lives **outside** the council through a multi-sectoral planning mechanism that include the voices and priorities of teachers, local businesses, cultural and community groups, and everyone. A citizenry then **elects** a local council that can implement the long-term plan.

Ensuring basic public services is never simply an administrative matter, rather an exercise in ensuring human rights.

The transformation from "subject" to "citizen" is the great unfinished narrative of human history. At its core, citizenship bears the principle of human dignity: every person has both the right and the responsibility to be the author of their own destiny.

A Global Team Effort

Participatory Local Democracy is inherently a team effort, and we greatly appreciate the active teamwork as well as the generous funding from the UN Democracy Fund (UNDEF) that makes this study possible.

At UNDEF's recommendation, we made our top priority for 2014 the empowerment of civil society organizations working on the frontlines of this issue as we collect data. We are deeply grateful to the following organizations who hosted the 34 multi-stakeholder focus groups in 32 countries this year – and to the hundreds of governmental, private sector and non-governmental organizations that sent representatives to these meetings.

Country	Organizer
Azerbaijan	Center for Economic and Social Development (CESD)
Bangladesh	THP Bangladesh
Cambodia	Cambodian Civil Society Partnership (CCSP)
Cameroon	Reflection and Concrete Actions for Africa Development (RECAAD)
Chile	Acción por la Tierra
Costa Rica	Fundación Ambio
Costa Rica	Paniamor
Cote d'Ivoire	Convention de la Société Ivoirienne (CSCI)
DR Congo	Save the Climat
Ethiopia	Association for Forced Migrants (AFM)
Guatemala	Acción Ciudadana
India	Institute of Social Sciences
Indonesia	Koalisi Perempuan Indonesia
Jordan	Al-Hayat Center for Civil Society Development
Kyrgyzstan	Global Civil Initiatives, Inc. (GCI)
Lebanon	Lebanese Foundation for Permanent Civil Peace (LFPCP)
Liberia	Youth Partnership for Peace and Development (YPPD)
Malawi	THP Malawi
Malaysia	Persatuan Aliran Kesedaran Negara (Aliran)
Mali	SOS Democratie
Mauritius	Allied Network for Policy, Research & Actions for Sustainability (ANPRAS)
Mexico	THP Mexico
Morocco	Center for Studies and Humanities Research (MADA)
Nepal	GoGo Foundation
Niger	YMCA Niger
Nigeria	Center for Democracy and Development (CDD)
Pakistan	Citizens' Commission on Human Development (CCHD)
Pakistan	Organization for Youth and Social Development (OYSD)
Paraguay	Semillas para la Democracia
Philippines	Local Government Development Foundation (LOGODEF)
Sierra Leone	Democracy Sierra Leone (DSL)
Sudan	Sudanese Development Initiative (SUDIA)
Tajikistan	Center for Civic Initiative
Uganda	THP Uganda

As we had hoped, the release of the 2013 report at numerous gatherings provided us with much helpful input, including events at the UN in partnership with the Mexican Government, at InterAction, the World Bank'sGlobal Partnership for Social Accountability, the OpenGovHub and the Konrad Adenauer Foundation in Berlin.

Production of the report also represents global teamwork, including our designer in India, Liza Cherian, our Spanish translator in Mexico City, Victoria Fuentes, and our French and Arabic translator in Paris, Rime Ech-chotbi. The survey was translated into French and Spanish by our staff colleague Margaux Yost and Ariadna Saavedra, respectively. The survey was translated into Russian by the organizer of our Kyrgyzstan meeting, Raissa Muhutdinova.

This report, and all the work of this project - to cultivate a global community of practice on Participatory Local Democracy - depended almost entirely on the next generation of international affairs professionals, including our project managers Mai Otake and Samirah Majumdar, our volunteers Anna Moriarty and Shanell Fan, and our interns over the past year: Tamene Adugna, Nan Huang, Clara Knutson and Karoline Kraft. As The Hunger Project staff members responsible – John Coonrod and Mary Kate Costello – responsibility for any errors or omissions falls solely with us.

AZERBAIJAN

PLDI rank	23
Population	9,295,784
HDI rank	82/187
HDI score	0.734

Azerbaijan enacted local self-government as one of the cornerstones of its constitutional system. The government established several laws aimed at increasing the powers of the municipalities. However, local self-authorities do not have sufficient capacity, training or knowledge to carry out such responsibilities (UCLG, 2009).

Local governance at a glance
- Azerbaijan is divided into 59 districts and 7 cities led by chairmen of municipalities and heads of structural divisions. Chairmen of municipalities are appointed by the president. Heads of structural divisions are selected by municipal councils (UCLG, 2009).
- The local government structure is comprised of two parallel systems of governance: publicly elected municipalities - with limited powers to deliver services to citizens, and Local Executive Authorities - appointed by the president and part of the state governing structure (Keymer, 2010).
- The number of municipality members is determined by law and differs depending on respective populations (UCLG, 2009).
- The Centre for the Work with Municipalities and a special department of the President's Office coordinate and oversee the national government's relationship with local governments (UCLG, 2009).
- Azerbaijan has no legislative gender quota at the subnational level (IDEA, 2013).

Civil society actors
- Election Monitoring and Democracy Studies Center (EMDS) is a non-partisan and independent non-governmental organization working for free and fair elections and the development of civil society and democratic traditions.
- Azerbaijan Youth Union (AYU) seeks to increase youth participation in civil society and democracy.

Capacity building institutions
- The Center of Municipal Reforms in Azerbaijan focuses on bringing together municipalities from different regions to form local government associations.
- The Academy of Public Administration (APA), established under the president's authority, provides training for civil servants such as informational technology for public administration.

Fiscal control
- Local governments have their own property and budgets as well as the right to impose local taxes and payments (UCLG, 2009).
- The central government allocates subsidies and subventions to the municipalities. Subsidies are used for equalization purposes and subventions finance social and economic development programs (Mikayilov, 2006).

Key initiatives for participatory local governance
- On November 12, 1995, local self-government received legal recognition in the Constitution for the first time (UCLG, 2009).
- In 1999, laws "On the Status of Municipalities" and "On the Elections of Municipalities" included the formation of a legal, normative basis for the organization and function of a local self-government system. Elections for local self-authorities were also held on a multi-party democratic basis for the first time (UCLG, 2009).
- Since 2000, 20 laws have been enacted to regulate different aspects of local government. These laws include "On the Status of Members of Municipalities," "On Joint Activities, Unification, Division and Liquidation of Municipalities," and "On Administrative Control over Activities of Municipalities" (UCLG, 2009).

Challenges for participatory local governance
- Although powers of the municipalities are increasing, the amount of subsidies from the central governments are decreasing yearly. Current revenue bases assigned to municipalities are insufficient to cover expenditures (UCLG, 2009).
- The number of responsibilities allocated to municipalities are limited by the law. In most cases municipalities do not have adequate capacity, training or knowledge to carry out those limited responsibilities prescribed by law (Keymer, 2010).
- The inclusion of NGOs in decision-making processes has been limited by insufficient development of the various democratic institutions (UNPAN, 2004).

List of sources:
The Academy of Public Administration, 2013: http://www.dia.edu.az/umumi2_en.php.
Azerbaijan Youth Union, 2009: http://www.ayu-az.org/en/2.html.
Election Monitoring and Democracy Studies Center (EMDS), 2014: http://www.gndem.org/emds
International Institute for Democracy and Electoral Assistance (IDEA), 2013: "Republic of Azerbaijan."
Keymer, G., Commission for Citizenship, Governance, Institutional and External Affairs, 2010: "Draft Opinion of the Commission for Citizenship, governance, Institutional and External Affairs on Local and Regional Government in Azerbaijan and the Development of Cooperation Between Azerbaijan and the EU."
Mamedova, M. and H. Bashir et al, 2002: "Local Government in Azerbaijan."
Mikayilov, E., 2006: "Intergovernmental Fiscal Transfers in Azerbaijan: Role of Tax- Sharing in Local Government Financing."
United Cities and Local Government (UCLG), 2009: "UCLG Country Profiles: Republic of Azerbaijan."
United Nations Public Administration Network (UNPAN), 2004: "Republic of Azerbaijan."

BANGLADESH

PLDI rank	13
Population	154,695,368
HDI rank	146/187
HDI score	0.515

Recent reforms of 2011 introduced mandatory mechanisms for citizen participation in local government. These include citizen charters, ward assemblies, five-year plans and the right to information (LGA, 2009).

Local governance at a glance

- Bangladesh has a four-tiered structure of governance: 7 regions (appointed), 64 districts (appointed), 484 upazilas (indirect elections) and 4,451 union parishads - or village clusters - (elected), of 9 wards (CLGF, 2011).
- The ten largest urban areas are administered as city corporations and 310 other urban municipalities are administered as paurashavas (CLGF, 2011).
- Members of the zila parishads are elected by an electoral college; five seats are reserved for women. There are also reserved seats for women in urban units, for which mayors and councilors are directly elected. Members of the upazila and union parishads are also directly elected. (CLGF, 2011).
- The Local Government Division is responsible for all local governments. The only exception is the hill district parishads, for which the Ministry of Hill Tract Affairs is responsible (CLGF, 2011).
- Three directly elected women's seats, each representing one of three wards, are added to each union parishad (Quota Project, 2014).

Civil society actors

- The Bangladesh Rural Advancement Committee (BRAC) seeks to build sustainable, social, accountability mechanisms through its Active Citizens and Accountable Local Government (ACALG) project. It works toward citizen participation, improvements in capacity of local government representatives, and increasing engagement between civil society, local government and the media (BRAC, 2013).
- SHUJAN, facilitated by The Hunger Project, is "organized at both the national and district levels to press for policy reforms to reduce corruption and strengthen local democracy" (THP, n.d.).

Capacity building institutions

- The Association of Union Parishads, the Association of Upazila Chairmen, and the Association of Paurashava are the three main associations of local government. They provide support to chairmen about their rights, privileges and welfare (CLGF, 2011).
- The National Institute of Local Government is the only [mandated] national level training and research institute of the local government. It is aimed at building the capacity of local government institutions focusing on the principles of good governance (NILG, 2012).

Fiscal control

- Although local governments collect revenue from income taxes, tolls, fees, rates, rents and profits from property, funding from the central government totals 90% of all local revenue (UCLG, 2010).

Key initiatives for participatory local governance

- Constitutional amendments made in 1972 and 2011 mandated that the state encourage "effective participation by the people through their elected representatives in administration at all levels" (Constitute Project, 2014).
- From 2000-2005, the Sirajganj Local Governance Development Fund Project (SLGFDP) piloted approaches to capacity building via block grants, social mobilization, public score cards, complaint books, open budget meetings, and ward-level bottom-up planning (World Bank, 2007).
- The SLGDFP mandated each Union Parishad to create five-year plans, form a budget through participatory processes and Open Budget Meetings, conduct two annual public assemblies for each ward, and publish a Citizen Charter (LGA, 2009).
- In 2007, the government and World Bank launched the Local Government Support Program followed in 2011 by the Union Parishad Governance Project and the Upazila Governance Project, both of which focus on strengthening local government to reduce poverty (UNCDF, 2013).
- In 2007, the Access to Information Programme was established to provide accessibility and transparency of the government via information and communications technology (THP, 2014).

Challenges for participatory local governance

- Each new leader who comes to power in Bangladesh attempts to nullify [all] efforts of the previous leader. This instability hinders significant progress in decentralization (Fox and Menon, 2008).
- Most local government employees are also central government employees. This prevents decentralized units from becoming truly established (Martinez-Vasquez and Vaillancourt, 2011).

List of sources:

Active Citizens and Accountable Local Government (ACALG), 2014: http://www.brac.net/content/community-empowerment-strengthening-local-governance#.VAYqfmRdWgd

BRAC, 2013: http://www.brac.net/content/what-we-do#.U8Auh1VX-nZ.

Commonwealth Local Government Forum (CLGF), 2011: "Country Profile: Bangladesh."

Constitute Project, 2014: "Bangladesh's Constitution of 1972, Reinstated in 1986, with Amendments through 2011."

Fox, W.F. and B. Menon, 2008: "Decentralization in Bangladesh: Change has been Illusive."

Local Government (UP) Act (LGA), 2009.

Martinez-Vasquez, J. and F. Vaillancourt, 2011: "Obstacles Decentralization: Lessons from the Developing World."

Quota Project, 2014: "Bangladesh."

The Hunger Project (THP), n.d.: www.thp.org/what_we_do/key_initiatives/fostering_government_accountability/overview.

The Hunger Project (THP), 2014: "Improving Access to Services through Technology in Bangladesh."

Trinamul Unnayan Sangstha (TUS), 2013: http://trinamulcht.org/?page_id=36.

United Cities and Local Governments (UCLG), 2010: "Local Government Finance: The Challenges of the 21st Century."

United Nations Capital Development Fund (UNCDF), 2014: "UNCDF in Bangladesh."

World Bank, 2007: "Empowering the Marginalized: Case Studies of Social Accountability Initiatives in Asia."

Decentralizing to Improve Democratic Participation in Bolivia
Professor Jean-Paul Faguet, London School of Economics

Citizen Engagement, Government Transparency and Accountability

In the early 1990s, Bolivia was mired in low growth and declining public faith in government. Allegations of corruption abounded. A new president decided that decentralization could permanently improve public sector efficiency, transparency and accountability to citizens. Devolving power and resources from a highly centralized national government to hundreds of local government bodies all over the country could increase citizen participation permanently.

The plan was broadly and strikingly successful. Public investment shifted dramatically in Bolivia towards social services like primary health and education, and away from big cities towards small, rural towns and villages. Citizen engagement in public decision-making rose markedly, both in terms of voter turnout and – more impressively – town hall meetings, public reporting of financial information and policy decisions, and active oversight by specially constituted bodies all over the country. Of the many reforms attempted during the 1990s, decentralization is the only one that was not only *not* subsequently reversed, but indeed was deepened considerably by Bolivia's current President Evo Morales, who "refounded" the republic with a new constitution.

The Pros and the Cons

In a nation that had lost half its original territory since independence, political elites feared decentralizing would stoke centrifugal forces that might split the country apart. Proponents of decentralization were mainly regional business elites in Santa Cruz, the business capital of Bolivia.- a region that had grown for decades at rates two to four times the national average. Railing against the "extraction" of local wealth by La Paz, local leaders appealed to regional identity and pride to demand more autonomy from the center and significantly larger royalties for the regional government they expected to dominate. Against them were also arrayed regional leaders from Bolivia's Western, poorer regions, who feared that power and fiscal resources would drain from them if the richer East gained significant autonomy.

How Did They Do It?

Reformers hit upon the idea of pulling the carpet out from under bullying elites who used secession as a political threat to extract fiscal resources. They could achieve this by decentralizing at the next level, below regions to Bolivia's municipalities. Instead of empowering potentially threatening business elites in Santa Cruz and elsewhere, these elites would be further disempowered by retaining unelected, weak regional administrations and instead creating more powerful, elected local governments throughout the country.

Why Did It Work?

As opposed to many countries where decentralization has been tried, reform worked in Bolivia with dramatic effects across the country's governance, public services, and politics. Why? Faguet (2012) identifies five main reasons:

1. **Sincere reform.** Decentralization was not just lip service or policy fashion. Bolivian reformers sincerely designed a reform to achieve it.

2. **Speed.** The reform law was announced in January and implemented on July 1st, 1994. Any reform proposing a major redistribution of power will face significant opposition from many who benefit from the status quo and stand to lose. Implementing reform slowly has few benefits in terms of municipal learning, but potentially large costs. By contrast, implementing reform quickly denies the opposition time to organize against reform.

3. **Simplicity and Transparency.** While other countries have imposed complicated transfer systems between center and periphery in the name of equity or efficiency, Bolivia used a simple per capita criterion. Although less efficient, per capita allocations made the financial implications of reform immediately obvious to a poorly educated population.

4. **Enhanced accountability** was built into the reform via Oversight Committees, which operate alongside municipal councils and the mayor. They in effect incorporate pre-existing social organizations (e.g. neighborhood councils, tribes, etc.) into municipal decision-making, thus boosting participation and legitimacy.

5. **Solution for Specific Political Problems.** The long-term decline of the MNR and other traditional parties, and the continuous threat of secession by the East were real threats that reoriented politicians' focus. In decentralization, those in power found a solution that they could embrace.

Further Readings

Faguet, J.P. 2012. *Decentralization and Popular Democracy: Governance from Below in Bolivia.* Ann Arbor: University of Michigan Press.

Faguet, J.P. and F. Sánchez. 2013. "Decentralization and Access to Social Services in Colombia." Public Choice. DOI 10.1007/s11127-013-0077-7.

Tendler, J. 1997. Good Government in the Tropics. Baltimore: Johns Hopkins University Press.

Treisman, D. 2007. The Architecture of Government: Rethinking Political Decentralization. New York: Cambridge University Press.

CAMBODIA

PLDI rank	11
Population	14,864,646
HDI rank	138/187
HDI score	0.543

After several decades of internal conflict, Cambodia has pursued decentralization policies. The process has been extended to provinces, or municipalities, and their district (khan) subdivisions (Smoke and Morrison, 2008).

Local governance at a glance
- Below the provincial and district levels are 1,630 elected commune and sangkat councils, or urban communes (UCLG, 2010).
- Established in 2008, the National Committee for Sub-National Democratic Development (NCDD) is the interministerial body that promotes democratic development through decentralization (NCDD, 2013).
- Local citizens directly elect representatives to the communes and sangkats. Those councils then elect District/Municipality and Provincial Councils (UCLG, 2011).
- While there are no legislated gender quotas, the government has committed to the Millenium Development Goal of promoting gender equality. The target is to increase female representation in the Commune (Sangkat) Councils to a minimum of 25% by the end of 2015 (CCHRC, 2012).

Civil society actors
- The Committee for Free and Fair Elections in Cambodia (COMFREL) works toward increasing citizen participation in local democratic development.
- Community Capacities for Development (CCD) focuses on capacity building at the grassroots level.
- The Cambodian Civil Society Partnership (CCSP) promotes decentralization and effective local governance.

Capacity building institutions
- The National League of Communes/Sangkats (NLC/S) is an association that works to enhance the status and capacity of Communes/Sangkat Councils, helping to create effective, transparent, sustainable, and self-reliant decentralized administrations.
- The Provincial Association of Commune/Sangkat Councils works toward the same goals at the provincial level of the government (UCLG, 2008).

Fiscal autonomy
- Communes account for less than 5 percent of total public expenditures (UCLG, 2010).
- The Law on Sub-National Fiscal Regime and Property Management passed in 2011. It aims to create sources of finance for sub-national government bodies to carry out local development (Cambodian National Budget, 2013).

Key initiatives for participatory local governance
- The National Program for Sub-National Democratic Development (NP-SNDD) was founded in 2008 as a ten year, comprehensive plan for governance reform of subnational administrations (NCDD, 2014).
- The government established an Organic Law on Decentralization and Democratic Development in 2009. This created indirectly elected councils at the provincial and district level (UCLG, 2010).
- Commune councils must prepare a five-year Development Plan as well as a three-year Investment Program. To achieve these plans, each council appoints a committee of male and female representatives from each village, commune councilors, and one representative from every NGO registered with the council (Smoke, 2008).

Challenges for participatory local governance
- Fiscal decentralization has been focused primarily on funding provisions for the communes with little emphasis on the reformation of provincial and municipal governance bodies (CDRI, 2011).
- Though the legal framework and overall strategy for decentralization has been established, there are few details on implementation (Smoke, 2008).
- Post-election violence in 2013, in which police attacked protesters, have been condemned as a "setback for democracy" by the global, bipartisan, and democracy-focused organization Freedom House (Freedom House, 2013).

List of sources:
Cambodian Center for Human Rights (CCHRC), 2012. "Female Political Representation and Electoral Gender Quota Systems."
The Cambodian Civil Society Partnership (CCSP), 2013: http://www.ccspcambodia.org/index.php/overview
Cambodian Development Resource Institute (CDRI), 2011. "Fiscal Decentralization in Cambodia: A Review of Progress and Changes."
The Cambodian National Budget, 2013. "Law on Public Finance."
Community Capacities for Development (CCD), n.d.: http://www.ccdcambodia.org/
Freedom House, 2013: "Post-election violence in Cambodia a setback for democracy."
The National Committee for Sub-National Democratic Development (NCDD), 2014. "National Program."
The National League of Communes/Sangkats, 2012: http://www.nlcs.org.kh/Page/EN/index.html
Smoke, P. and Morrison, J., International Center for Public Policy, Andrew Young School of Policy Studies, 2008. "Decentralization in Cambodia: Consolidating Central Power or Building Accountability from Below?"
United Cities and Local Governments (UCLG), 2010: "Local Government Finance: The Challenges of the 21st Century."
United Cities and Local Governments (UCLG), 2008. "Asia Pacific."

CAMEROON

PLDI rank	48
Population	29,699,631
HDI rank	150/187
HDI score	0.495

Cameroon continues to make progress in transferring responsibilities to the local level. However, fiscal decentralization, a lack of local capacity, and the absence of a strong civil society continue to challenge the process (GIZ, n.d.).

Local governance at a glance

- Cameroon is divided into 10 administrative regions, each divided into divisions, and divisions into sub-divisions. The number of local governments amounts to 376 councils, including 14 city councils, and 42 sub-divisional councils within the cities (CLGF, 2013).
- Councillors are elected via universal suffrage for a five-year term. Councils and sub-division councils are headed by a mayor directly elected by councillors, whereas city councils are headed by a government body appointed by the president (CLGF, 2013).
- The Ministry of Territorial Administration and Decentralization (MINATD) is responsible for relations between the central and local government. It also oversees the regional and local authorities and their decentralization policies (CLGF, 2013).
- Cameroon does not have gender quotas at the subnational level (Quota Project, 2013).

Civil society actors

- Reflection and Concrete Actions for Africa Development (RECAAD-Cameroon) seeks to promote good governance, and fights for human rights and the eradication of corruption (RECAAD-Cameroon, 2014).
- The Zenü Network consists of several civil society actors that work with regional and local authorities as well as associations and movements to identify and strengthen local governance (Zenü Network, 2012).

Capacity building institutions

- The Local Government Training Centre is a training center for current and new local government officials and staff. It is supervised by the MINATD (CLGF, 2013).
- United Councils and Cities of Cameroon (UCCC) is an association of all of Cameroon's councils that seeks to contribute to the process of decentralization. It supports its members with financial assistance and capacity-building among other things (UCCC, 2014).

Fiscal control

- Local authorities can raise taxes and charges an annual business levy up to US$200 (CLGF, 2013).
- The local budget derives from transfers from the central government through the MINATD via the Special Council Support Fund for Mutual Assistance (FEICOM) (CLGF, 2013).

Key initiatives for participatory local governance

- The 1972 Constitution and the Poverty Reduction Strategy of 2009 both identify local governance as a means of improving service delivery, accountability of officials, regional tensions, inclusion, and environmental management (World Bank, 2012).
- The 1996 Constitution recognizes the decentralized nature of the state and officially established regions as both regional and local authority (Constitution of Cameroon, 1996).
- In 2004, several laws were passed to finally lay down a [former] legal framework for decentralisation, which included a transfer of powers to local entities. This devolution included financial, material and human means as well as the establishment of the National Council for Decentralization, and an Interministerial Committee for Local Services (Cheka, 2007).

Challenges for participatory local governance

- The World Bank stated that Cameroon's "legal framework relating to decentralization is overlapping, (...) contradictory, and in many respects open to different interpretations. The main difficulty is that decentralized functions are ill-defined and not distinct from 'deconcentrated' operations of the central government" (World Bank, 2012).
- Despite strong decentralization legislation, Cameroon lacks an effective strategy and operational plan for decentralization (World Bank, 2012).
- The small budgets of municipalities often lead to a lack of qualified staff to exercise tasks properly (Desbrosses, 2014).
- In 2008, constitutional amendments provided for an intermediary provincial level of local government. However, this has not yet been realized (CLGF, 2013).

List of sources:

Cheka, C., 2007, African Development: "The State of the Process of Decentralisation in Cameroon."

Commonwealth Local Government Forum (CLGF), 2013: "Country Profile: The local government system in Cameroon."

Constitution of the Republic of Cameroon, 1996: http://confinder.richmond.edu/admin/docs/Cameroon.pdf.

Desbrosses, A., 2014, WikiTerritorial du CNFPT: "La décentralisation au Cameroun: un goût d'inachevé."

Deutsche Gesellschaft fur Internationale Zusammenarbeit (GIZ), n.d.: "Cameroon."

United Councils and Cities of Cameroon (UCCC), 2014: www.cvuc.cm/national/index.php/en.

Quota Project, 2013: "Cameroon."

Reflection and Concrete Actions for Africa Development (RECAAD-Cameroon), 2014: www.unodc.org/ngo/showSingleDetailed.do?req_org_uid=21764.

World Bank, 2012: "Cameroon - The Path to Fiscal Decentralization: Opportunities and Challenges."

Zenü Network, 2012: www.zenu.org/spip.php.

PLDI rank	37
Population	17,464,814
HDI rank	40/187
HDI score	0.819

The history of military rule in Chile contributed to its decentralization process, as several responsibilities were transferred to the municipalities in the 1980s. Their recent history of democracy began in 1992, when the country held its first democratic elections for local leadership. (UCLG, 2007).

Local governance at a glance

- The country is divided into 15 regions, each led by an executive officer appointed by the regional council (UCLG, 2010).
- The 345 municipalities are lead by popularly elected mayors and councilors (UCLG, 2010).
- The Ministry of the Interior maintains responsibility for local authorities (UCLG, 2010).
- Chile does not have legislated local gender quotas (Quota Project, 2014).

Civil society actors

- Action for the Earth promotes citizen participation and transparency for environmental and developmental issues affecting Chile (Action for the Earth, 2014).
- Corporacion Proyectamérica is a center for dialogue and information exchange within civil society (Poderopedia, 2013).

Capacity building institutions

- The Chilean Association of Municipalities represents the municipalities to assist with decentralization efforts and improve citizen access to participatory practices (AChM, 2013).
- The Secretariat for Regional and Administrative Development (SUBDERE) helps develop regions and municipalities by strengthening their capacity for good governance.

Fiscal control

- In past years, the federal government transferred 13.2% of total revenue to the municipal governments (UCLG, 2007).
- Local government expenditures in Chile are 12.8% of total government expenditure, or 2.4% of GDP (UCLG, 2007).
- The local governments are allocated urban property, alcohol, and car registration taxes, as well as revenue from public utility, fines, and permit fees. They are also allowed to set tax rates and change tax bases in accordance to legal limitations (UCLG, 2010).

Key initiatives for participatory local governance

- The educational decentralization program of the 1980s shifted control of public schools to the hands of private institutions. This resulted in stronger, quality education as schools competed for students and families became more invested in the schools (World Bank, 2004).

- In 2005, the Chilean Association of Municipalities initiated a municipal reform to broaden the scope of governance for municipal administrators and promote collaboration between municipal governments. This proposed an increase in spending on local governments to 30% of the total national revenue (UCLG, 2007).

Challenges for participatory local governance

- Chilean municipalities are limited by dependence on the federal government. There are limited funds for municipalities, and local governments do not have the resources to successfully complete the jobs set before them (UCLG, 2007).
- The UNDP's assessment of their work in Chile from 2001 to 2009 states that the goal to "advance decentralization" has yet to be significantly realized (UNDP, 2010).

List of sources:
Action for the Earth, 2014: http://www.accionporlatierra.cl/.
Chilean Association of Muncipalities (AChM), 2013: http://www.achm.cl/.
Poderopedia, 2012: http://www.poderopedia.org/cl/organizaciones/Corporacion_ProyectAmerica.
Quota Project, 2014: "Chile."
Secretariat for Regional and Administrative Development: http://www.subdere.gov.cl/.
United Nations Development Program (UNDP), 2010: "Executive Summary."
United Cities and Local Governments (UCLG), 2007: "Country Profile: Republic of Chile."
United Cities and Local Governments (UCLG), 2010: "Local Government Finance: The Challenges of the 21st Century."
World Bank, 2004: "Education Decentralization and Accountability Relationships in Latin America."

COSTA RICA

PLDI rank	21
Population	4,805,295
HDI rank	62/187
HDI score	0.773

Costa Rica has long been recognized for having one of the most centralized systems of governance in Central America. Since the early 2000s, the government has taken steps to promote decentralization, including a landmark 2010 fiscal decentralization law (Long, 2010).

Local governance at a glance

- The country is divided into seven provinces, each led by a governor appointed by the president. Provinces are divided into 81 counties (cantones) with local mayors (Encyclopedia Britannica, 2013).
- Municipal district (districtos) councils are popularly elected (UCLG, 2007).
- Local governance is overseen by the National Finance and Accounts Office, the Treasury Department, the Institute of Municipal Promotion and Evaluation, and sometimes the Presidential Ministry (UCLG, 2007).
- According to the 2009 candidate quota law, 50% of candidates on a party list must be female and two people of the same sex may not be listed subsequently. Electoral authorities can reject lists that do not comply (Quota Project, 2014).

Civil society actors

- Young Citizens in Action is a project supported by the Paniamor Foundation and the UN Democracy Fund to strengthen young people's participation in local decisionmaking (Paniamor Foundation, n.d.).
- DEMUCA Foundation strengthens municipal administration by creating technical units that support activities for which they have insufficient funds (DEMUCA Foundation, 2014).

Capacity building institutions

- The National Union of Local Governments (UNGL) provides training through seminars and workshops to support municipal management (UNGL, 2014).
- The Institute for Municipal Capacity and Training and Local Development at Universidad Estatal a Distancia (UNED) strengthens municipal authorities through trainings on municipal and community development management (UNED, n.d.).

Fiscal control

- Municipalities collect taxes to use for public services, but Congress must approve local taxes (UCLG, 2010).
- A 2010 law mandated that the central government transfer at least 10% of federal funds to the local level by 2017 and ensure that local entities have the capacity to administer these funds appropriately (Long, 2010).

Key initiatives for participatory local governance

- The central government created several reforms in the late 1990's including the Municipal Code, which promotes decentralization and citizen participation (Ryan, 2012):
  - The municipal executive elections shifted to a popular election wherein voters must approve any changes to municipal regulations or practices.
  - Open meetings (cabildos) provide a public forum about decisions or issues in a district or municipality.
  - Mayors are annually required to make a public outline of local government priorities.
  - In 2010, a law was passed to strengthen municipalities and provide them with more financial resources (Long, 2010).

Challenges for participatory local governance

- Many municipalities have limited financial management without regulations for administering taxes (ICMA, 2004).
- A lack of funding has halted the establishment of set regulations for proper municipal government training (ICMA, 2004).
- Limited accountability and missing development plans are leading to a lack of result-oriented municipal planning (ICMA, 2004).

List of sources:

Demuca Foundation, 2014: http://www.demuca.org/.

Encyclopedia Britannica, 2013: "Costa Rica."

International City/County Management Association (ICMA), 2004: "Costa Rica Country Report: Trends in Decentralization, Municipal Strengthening, and Citizen Participation in Central America, 1995-2003."

National Union of Local Governments (UNGL), 2014: http://www.ungl.or.cr/.

Paniamor Foundation, n.d.: http://paniamor.org/Jovenes-Ciudadanos-En-Accion/undef.

Quota Project, 2014: "Costa Rica."

Ryan, J., 2012, Latin American Policy: "Decentralization in Costa Rica: The Effects of Reform on Participation and Accountability."

Long, C., 2010, The Tico Times: "Bill to Strengthen Municipalities Signed into Law."

UN Democracy Fund (UNDEF), n.d.: http://www.un.org/democracyfund/

United Cities and Local Government (UCLG), 2007: "Country Profile: Republic of Costa Rica."

United Cities and Local Governments (UCLG), 2010: "Local Government Finance: The Challenges of the 21st Century."

Universidad Estatal a Distancia (UNED), n.d.: http://www.uned.ac.cr/ifcmdl/index.php?option=com_content&view=article&id=130&Itemid=207

CÔTE D'IVOIRE

PLDI rank	32
Population	20,316,086
HDI rank	168/187
HDI score	0.432

There has been a significant presence of political instability and violence over the last decade, including a civil war in 2002 and an outbreak of violence after elections in 2010 and 2013. This uncertainty has led to inconsistent implementation of fiscal and administrative reforms, especially at the local level (Freedom House, 2014; UCLG, 2008b).

Local governance at a glance
- Côte d'Ivoire is divided into 31 provinces, 81 departments, and 197 communes (DGDDL, 2010).
- Municipal councils are directly elected for five-year terms. Local executives are indirectly appointed (UCLG, 2010).
- Municipalities are responsible for social assistance (UCLG, 2010).
- At the national level the General Directorate of Decentralization and Local Development (DGDDL), within the Ministry of State, Interior and Security, is responsible for monitoring devolution and oversight of local goverments' financial support, capacity building and technical support (DGDDL, 2010).
- Côte d'Ivoire does not have legislated gender quotas at the subnational level (Quota Project, 2013).

Civil society actors
- The Coalition de la Société Civile pour la Paix et le développement démocratique en Côte d'Ivoire (COSOPCI) is an organization that works to strengthen social cohesion and accountability through the promotion of post conflict reconciliation. This includes training locally elected leaders on good governance and civil society engagement (COSOPCI, 2010).
- The Centre de Recherche et d'action pour la paix (CERAP) works on human rights issues via social action, publications, and capacity building training (CERAP, 2014).

Capacity building institutions
- The Union des Villes et Communes de Côte d'Ivoire (UVICOCI) was established in 1993 by municipal leaders to help instrument the government's decentralization policy (UVICOCI, n.d.).

Fiscal control
- The local government does not collect taxes, but can change rates and receives a share of the central government's tax revenue (UCLG, 2008a).
- In 2007, the local governments' expenditures were estimated to have been 11% of the total government expenditure (UCLG, 2010).
- The Loan Fund for Local Authorities (Fonds de Pret aux Collectivites Locales FPCL) makes loans to local governments and is capitalized by the central government and the international community (UCLG, 2010).

Key initiatives for participatory local governance
- In 2002, the country held its first election for departmental councils (UNPAN, 2007).
- In 2010, violence and major political crises occurred after President Gbagbo refused to step down after the election. By 2011, the country recovered enough to hold successful legislative elections (IMF, 2012).
- From 2009 to 2013 the Government achieved the following:
  - A draft of local development plans with local participation
  - Training of female local leaders in leadership, and participatory planning
  - Dissemination of the local participatory planning manual developed by the Ministry of State and the Ministry of Planning and Development (IMF, 2012).
- There were local and regional elections in 2013, marking progress in the country's gradual return to normal multiparty political activity (Freedom House, 2014).

Challenges for participatory local governance
- The 2012 country plan jointly developed by the IMF and the Government of Côte d'Ivoire describes the following challenges:
  - Low overall citizen involvement in local community management
  - An absence of a consistent decentralization strategy with resources to finance its development and execution (IMF, 2012).
- Transparency International's corruption measurement ranked Côte d'Ivoire very low due to high levels of corruption in the country (Freedom House, 2014).

List of sources:
Centre de Recherche et d'action pour la paix (CERAP), 2014: http://www.cerap-inades.org/.
Coalition de la Société Civile pour la Paix et le développement démocratique en Côte d'Ivoire (COSOPCI), 2010: http://www.cosopci-ci.org/.
Direction Generale de la Decentralisation et du Developpement Local (DGDLL), 2010: "Missions et Attributions."
Freedom House, 2014: "Côte d'Ivoire."
International Monetary Fund (IMF), 2012: "Côte d'Ivoire: Poverty Reduction Strategy Paper Progress Report."
Union des Villes et Communes de Côte d'Ivoire (UVICOCI), n.d.: http://2gwebhost.com/templates_sav/uvicoci/statut.html.
United Cities and Local Governments (UCLG), 2008a: "Decentralization and local democracy in the world."
United Cities and Local Governments (UCLG), 2008b: "Republic of Côte d'Ivoire."
United Cities and Local Governments (UCLG), 2010: "Local Government Finance: The Challenges of the 21st Century."
United Nations Public Administration Network (UNPAN), 2007: "Côte d'Ivoire: Public Administration Country Profile."
Quota Project, 2013: "Côte d'Ivoire."

DEMOCRATIC REPUBLIC OF THE CONGO

PLDI rank	13
Population	65,705,093
HDI rank	186/187
HDI score	0.304

A new Constitution went into effect in 2006. This was an important step toward more decentralization in the Democratic Republic of the Congo (DRC). However, the past few years have been marked by surges in violence and failure to implement decentralization reforms called for by the Constitution.

Local governance at a glance

- The new Constitution maintained the existing 11 provinces, but directed that they be divided into 26 within three years. To date, this has not occurred (SSRC, 2013).
- Provinces are further subdivided into Decentralized Territorial Entities (ETDs): cities, communes, sectors and chefferies (DRC Constitution, 2005).
- The Ministry of Decentralization and Territorial Organization was created by the 2006 Constitution to oversee decentralization. However, it was eliminated in 2011 by a presidential decree (SSRC, 2013).
- The Constitution called for directly elected assemblies at the national, provincial and local levels. However, the ETDs do not have elected assemblies and the administrators are appointed by the president (SSRC, 2013).
- The Constitution states the right of women "to equal representation in national, provincial and local institutions." However, there is no provision of sanctions in cases of non-compliance (Quota Project, 2014).

Civil society actors

- Observatory for the Freedom of the Press in Africa is a network of journalists and legal experts that promote freedom of the press throughout the DRC (Societecivile, 2014).
- S.O.S. Climat seeks to educate people and raise awareness about climate change and the importance of protecting the environment (S.O.S. Climat, 2014).

Capacity building initiatives

- The World Bank Institute's ICT4Gov program has introduced mobile technology to enhance participatory budgeting processes (World Bank, 2012).

Fiscal control

- The 2006 Constitution established that provinces would receive 40% of tax revenue. Of this amount, they would then allocate 10% to an equalization fund and 40% to the ETDs. This was determined by a formula that accounts for production capacity, land area, and population. To date, this has not occurred (World Bank, 2011a).

Key initiatives for participatory local governance

- The country's 2006 presidential, national assembly and provincial assembly elections were the first multi-party elections in 46 years.
- The 2006 Constitution was an important step towards a more decentralized system: provide provinces with a better budget, re-devide the provinces, and call for the establishment of elected assemblies on all levels. However, little has been done (SSRC, 2013).
- In 2009, the country released a plan dividing decentralization into two phases. The first phase (2009-2014) would establish the necessary political conditions for the provinces and the ETDs, including local elections and the further territorial division. The second phase (2015-2019) would be devoted to strengthening the process of decentralization (SSRC, 2013).

Challenges for participatory local governance

- The ETDs are ineffective at "providing public goods and services to their populations" and have a lack of "internal management of resources (…), which results in the absence of budgets and financial reports." ETDs are further characterized "by the lack of a structured administrative organization", such as "under-qualified (…) staff, weak technical capacity and a lack of infrastructure" (World Bank, 2011a).
- Concurrent provincial elections have continually been delayed since 2006 and local elections have not been held. The failure to instrument the 2006 Constitution and hold elections has been a major hindrance to furthering decentralization (World Bank, 2011b).
- Provinces transfer funds to ETDs irregularly and informally at provincial authorities' discretion (World Bank, 2011a).

List of sources:
Constitution of the Democratic Republic of the Congo (DRC Constitution), 2005: http://www.constitutionnet.org/files/DRC%20-%20Congo%20Constitution.pdf.
S.O.S. Climat, 2014. "About."
Quota Project, 2014: "Democratic Republic of the Congo."
Social Science Research Council (SSRC), 2013, Weiss, H. and G. Nzongola-Ntalaja: "Decentralization and the DRC – An Overview."
Societecivile.cd, 2014: "Observatoire de la Liberté de la Presse en Afrique (OLPA)."
World Bank, 2011a: "Democratic Republic of Congo – An Analysis of Administrative, Financial, and Public Service Delivery Status in Decentralized Territorial Entities (ETDs)."
World Bank, 2011b, Gambino, T.: "World Development Report 2011. Democratic Republic of the Congo."
World Bank, 2012, Estefan, F. and B. Weber: "Mobile Enhanced Participatory Budgeting in DRC."

PLDI rank	3
Population	91,728,849
HDI rank	173/187
HDI score	0.396

Ethiopia was a centralized country in the 19th and 20th centuries. In the past two decades, it has experienced two rounds of decentralization that have led to changes in political, fiscal and administrative areas (USAID, 2010).

Local governance at a glance

- Ethiopia is a federal republic with five administrative tiers: federal, regional, zonal, district (woredas), and village areas (kebele) (IFPRI, 2011).
- There are nine regional governments and two city administrations. At the zonal level, cabinets are appointed by the regional government in all but one zone. At the district woreda level in rural areas, representative councils are directly elected by local people. Representative councils appoint executive and judicial bodies in urban woredas and city administrations (USAID, 2010).
- Ethiopia does not have legislative gender quotas. However, the current rule for the running party provides for a 30% quota (IDEA, 2012).

Civil society actors

- Vision Ethiopian Congress for Democracy (VECOD) promotes awareness of democratic citizenship, democratic governance and leadership, and provides training courses on leadership, civic education and management skills (VECOD, n.d.).
- The Ethiopian International Institute for Peace & Development (EIIPD) offers civic and voter education trainings that focus on indicators of democratic governance, participatory politics, and gender equality in governance (EIIPD, 2014).

Capacity building institutions

- The Ethiopian Civil Service University (ECSU) offers consultancies and academic training on decentralization, municipal finance, public service delivery and good governance at the federal and regional levels (ECSU, 2010).
- The 2006 Promoting Basic Services Program improves access to basic services, strengthens the "decentralized public financial management system," and creates avenues through which citizens can provide feedback to local administrators about service delivery (World Bank, 2013).

Fiscal control

- Regional and district-level governments receive block grant transfers from one government level higher. These funds are their most important source of financing and are "for addressing the vertical imbalances in revenue versus expenditure assignments between the federal and regional administrations" (World Bank, 2008).
- The allocation of federal funds vary by region as they are based on needs and revenue potential (USAID, 2010).

Key initiatives for participatory local governance

- In 1992, Ethiopia's transitional government initiated decentralization by devolving "significant administrative responsibilities" to regions, giving them "substantial discretionary authority" to implement policies made by the central government (IFPRI, 2011).
- In the first phase, a four-tier governance structure (center, regions, zones, and districts) was created. The regional governments were made responsible for delivering public services such as education and health (World Bank, 2008).
- The delivery of basic services improved when "massive decentralization of fiscal resources" to the regions took place in 1994 and to the woredas between 2002 and 2003 (World Bank, 2008).
- In 2002 and 2003, district governments in four of the largest regions were given more responsibility over public goods and services, and planning and budgeting (IFPRI, 2011).

Challenges for participatory local governance

- Many districts lack capacity, skilled personnel, and infrastructure to support progress in water, electricity, and communication networks (World Bank, 2008).
- District administrations "rely almost exclusively on unconditional block grants from regional governments. About 90% of these grants are spent on salaries and operational costs." Little is invested in service delivery (World Bank, 2008).
- Revenue collection is centralized, while expenditures are decentralized. This gives the central government leverage over regional spending (USAID, 2010).

List of sources:
Ethiopian Civil Service University (ECSU), 2010: http://www.ecsc.edu.et/.
Ethiopian International Institute for Peace & Development (EIIPD), 2014: http://eiipdethiopia.org/.
International Institute for Democratic and Electoral Assistance (IDEA), 2012: "Ethiopia."
International Food Policy Research Institute (IFPRI), 2011, Cohen, M. and M. Lemma: "Agricultural Extension Services and Gender Equality."
United States Agency for International Development (USAID), 2010: "Comparative Assessment of Decentralization in Africa: Ethiopia Desk Study."
Vision Ethiopian Congress for Democracy (VECOD), n.d.: http://www.vecod.org.et/.
World Bank, 2008, Garcia, M. and A. Rajkumar: "Achieving Better Service Delivery through Decentralization in Ethiopia."
World Bank, 2013: "Q&A: Ethiopia's Promoting Basic Services (PBS) III Program."

PLDI rank	25
Population	15,082,831
HDI rank	133/187
HDI score	0.581

Decentralization efforts in Guatemala have yielded a better balance of power and stronger, independent local governments. However, a low budget and small transfer of funds from the central government hampers municipal development (UCLG, 2008).

Local governance at a glance

- The country is divided into 22 departments and 332 municipalities. Each department is governed by a Departmental Council for Development, elected by a majority vote. A governor, chosen by the president, oversees the councils. Municipalities are governed by an elected municipal council and a mayor, who is directly elected by the people (UCLG, 2008).
- At the national level, government officials from the Secretary of the Presidency address issues relating to decentralization on a monthly basis. The Ministry of the Interior oversees the authority of local governments (World Bank, 2005; UCLG, 2008).
- Guatemala has no legislated subnational gender quotas (Quota Project, 2014).

Civil society actors

- The Association of Investigation and Social Studies (ASIES) supports activities that promote public participation. The association is a national forum for citizens to reflect on and discuss political, social and economic concepts (ASIES, 2012).
- Citizen Action is a branch of Transparency International that seeks to combat corruption in Guatemala and promote democracy and citizen participation (Citizen Action, 2012).

Capacity building institutions

- The Guatemalan Association of Indigenous Mayors and Authorities (AGAAI) focuses on strengthening municipalities, promoting gender equity and supporting indigenous communities (AGAAI, 2010).
- The National Association of Municipalities of Guatemala (ANAM) is a private entity whose mission is to strengthen municipalities and promote local leadership (ANAM, n.d.).

Fiscal control

- Municipalities' budgets are composed of their own limited revenues collected through taxes and transfers from the central government. The 1985 Constitution states that 10% of general revenue from the central government must be transferred to municipalities (World Bank, 2013).

Key initiatives for participatory local governance

- When Guatemala returned to democracy in 1994, a new Constitution was devised by May of 1985. This started the decentralization process, defining "decentralization as an administrative and economic reform that should be based on citizen participation" (Ruano, 2012). Key laws and reforms regarding decentralization resulted from the Peace Accords of 1996 (Ruano, 2012).
- In 2002, a Law of Decentralization, a revision of the Municipal Code, and a new social development council system were passed. This set of laws transferred powers and responsibilities to municipalities and other executive branches (Ruano, 2012).
- The Guatemala Decentralization Forum, started in 2005, provides an organized agenda for government authorities to come together, discuss the challenges facing decentralization and meet different experts (World Bank, 2005).
- The Guatemala Municipal Radio Training Program is a World Bank initiative aimed at improving Guatemala's decentralization policy. The courses educate citizens - particularly community leaders, government officials and people interested in participating in the local government - about the law, how to formulate public requests, and make municipal investments (World Bank, 2007).

Challenges for participatory local governance

- Municipalities face financial challenges: congress determines taxes, they are dependent on transfers from the central government, and their budgets tend to be small (UCLG, 2008; World Bank, 2013).
- Corruption remains a serious problem. In the Corruption Perception Index 2013, Transparency International ranked Guatemala 123rd out of 177 countries (TI, 2013).
- An increase in organized crime has put the stability of different regions and the state at risk (USAID, 2014).

List of sources:

Association of Investigation and Social Studies (ASIES), 2012: http://www.asies.org.gt.

Citizen Action, 2012: http://www.accionciudadana.org.gt.

Guatemalan Association of Indigenous Mayors and Authorities (AGAAI), 2010: http://notiagaai.blogspot.com/p/agaai.html.

National Association of Municipalities of Guatemala (ANAM), n.d.: http://anam.org.gt/nueva/.

Quota Project, 2014: "Guatemala."

Ruano, A., 2012: "The role of social participation in municipal-level health systems: the case of Palencia, Guatemala."

Transparency International (TI), 2013: "Corruption by country/territory. Guatemala."

United Cities and Local Governments (UCLG), 2008: "Republic of Guatemala country profile."

USAID, 2014: "Guatemala. Democracy and Governance."

World Bank, 2005: "The Guatemala Decentralization Forum."

World Bank, 2007: "Guatemala Municipal Radio Training Program."

World Bank, 2013: "Towards Better Expenditure Quality. Guatemala Public Expenditure Review."

PLDI rank	25
Population	1,236,686,732
HDI rank	136/187
HDI score	0.554

India's constitution calls for strongly decentralized, participatory local democracy. However, the state governments often refrain from transferring power to the local level (Rao and Raghunandan, et al., 2011).

Local governance at a glance

- India is a federal republic with central, state, and local governments. It is comprised of 28 states and seven union territories, which are governed by the central government. The local government is divided into urban authorities (municipalities) and rural authorities (panchayats) (UCLG, 2007; CLGF, 2013).
- Three types of municipalities exist. A nagar panchayat is in transition from rural to urban, municipal councils are smaller urban areas, and municipal corporations are larger urban areas (CLGF, 2013).
- In most states, the panchayat system is a three-tiered structure: village, intermediate and district. At the village level, citizens elect their governing council (gram panchayat) and its chairperson, who serves on the intermediate panchayat council. The intermediate panchayat council elects representatives to the district panchayat (Encyclopedia Britannica, 2013).
- State municipal law mandates that urban municipalities with over 300,000 people must elect ward committees led by councilors (CLGF, 2013).
- The task of devolving power and developing local institutions lies with the state. Local governments are under the control of state governments, whose governor is appointed by the president (UCLG, 2007).
- According to the Constitution, 33% of all seats within local government bodies must be reserved for women. Some states have raised this quota to half of all seats in their panchayats and municipalities (Quota Project, 2014).

Civil society actors

- The Society for the Promotion of Area Resource Centers (SPARC) fosters community participation with local authorities to meet the challenges of urban population growth (SPARC, n.d.).
- All India Institute of Local Self-Government (AIILSG) is an autonomous research and training institution to strengthen urban local governance, share best practices, and provide capacity building and training (AIILSG, 2014).

Capacity building institutions

- Created in 2007, the Decentralization Community of Practice (CoP) brings together individuals focused on strengthening local governance. Foci include political, functional, administrative and financial decentralization for urban and rural areas. It is hosted by UNDP's Democratic Governance Unit (CoP, 2011).
- The National Council of Applied Economic Research (NCAER) analyzes aspects of rural governance to determine the effectiveness of decentralization and government institutions at achieving inclusive and poverty-alleviating growth (NCAER, 2012).

Fiscal control

- Local governments can impose taxes, user fees, and other charges. Municipalities' property taxes account for nearly 60% of their revenue and some cities levy taxes on incoming goods. Panchayats receive intergovernmental transfers, which account for approximately 90% of rural panchayat revenue (UCLG, 2007; Rao and Raghunandan et al., 2011).
- Most urban infrastructure projects undertaken by municipal local governments depend primarily on funds from state governments and other agencies (CLGF, 2013).

Key initiatives for participatory local governance

- In 1992, the 73rd and 74th constitutional amendments passed. They called for the creation of the three-tier local government structure, direct elections in urban and rural areas, greater political and fiscal authority for panchayats, and reserved seats for Scheduled Castes and Scheduled Tribes (UCLG, 2007; World Bank, 2013).
- In 2010, India implemented the Centralized Public Grievance Redress and Monitoring System for citizen complaints. Through this accountability mechanism, citizens can submit grievances and subsequently track progress toward them (Zeenews, 2012).
- Every year, the Ministry of Panchayati Raj (MPR) assesses states' devolution and publishes rankings on the MPR website (MPR, 2014).

Challenges for participatory local governance

- States have been restrained to transfer powers to local governments (Rao and Raghunandan, et al., 2011).
- "Despite Constitutional recognition, the design and implementation of rural decentralization do not enable the panchayats to be the institutions of rural self government" (Rao and Raghunandan et al., 2011).
- In order to act as a functional institution of self government, panchayats need "a greater degree of political willingness & effective fiscal devolution" (Mohapatra, 2012).

List of sources:
All India Institute of Local Self-Government (AIILSG), 2014: http://www.aiilsg.org/.
Commonwealth Local Government Forum (CLGF), 2013: "Country Profile: India."
Encyclopedia Britannica, 2013: "India. State and local governments."
United Cities and Local Governments (UCLG), 2007: "UCLG Country Profiles: Republic of India."
Ministry of Panchayati Raj (MPR), 2014: "Ranking of States/UTS based Devolution of Funds, Functions and Functionaries to PRIS."
Mohapatra, B., 2012: "Local Self-Governing Institutions and Fiscal

Decentralisation in India: Form to Function."

National Council of Applied Economic Research (NCAER), 2012: http://www.ruralgov-ncaer.org/index.php.

Quota Project, 2014: "India."

Rao, M., and T. Raghunandan et al., 2011: "Fiscal Decentralization to Rural Local Governments in India: Selected Issues and Reform Options."

Society for the Promotion of Area Resource Centers (SPARC), n.d.: http://www.sparcindia.org/.

World Bank, 2013, Mansuri, G. and V. Rao: "Localizing Development. Does Participation Work?"

Decentralization Community of Practice (CoP), 2011: www.in.undp.org/content/india/en/home/ourwork/democraticgovernance/decentralization-community--solution-exchange-india/.

Zeenews.com, 2012: "Over 27,000 public grievances received in 2011."

INDONESIA

PLDI rank	6
Population	246,864,191
HDI rank	121/187
HDI score	0.629

Indonesia has pursued a method for decentralization reforms that have come to be called the "big bang." There has been a relatively dramatic devolution of most government functions from the highly centralized state to the district level (World Bank, 2002).

Local governance at a glance

- Local and provincial governments are autonomous, administrative, and territorial bodies within the unitary state. At the subnational level, Indonesia is divided into provincial and city, or district levels, each with their own legislative bodies and government system (World Bank, 2006).
- The local parliament is led by a governor, city governments by a mayor, and district governments by a regent. Mayors and governors are directly elected (World Bank, 2006).
- The Ministry of the Interior oversees the local governments and the Ministry of Finance and Supreme Audit Board is responsible for finances (UCLG, 2007).
- Women must make up 30% of the nominees for members of the People's Representative Council and Regional House of Representatives at the subnational level (Quota Project, 2014).

Civil society actors

- The Partnership for Governance Reform (Kemitraan) works to advance good governance, transparency, decentralization and an empowered civil society within government, civil society and the private sector (Kemitraan, 2014).
- Satunama is an organization that works to promote transparency, accountability and anti-corruption in governance by building networks and strengthening cooperation among individuals, organizations, and communities (Satunama, 2011).

Capacity building institutions

- The Association of Indonesian Municipalities (APEKSI) conducts capacity building activities for city governments, including themes covering local finance, civil service reforms, corruption, and "gender responsive planning and budgeting" (APEKSI, 2014).
- The Indonesian Municipal Councils Association (ADEKSI) consists of 93 municipal councils and provides them with workshops on good governance. ADEKSI also consults municipal councils on drafting and implementing local regulations with public participation (DELGOSEA, 2014).

Fiscal control

- Law 25/1999 requires the central government to transfer at least 25% of domestic net revenues to the subnational level. Of this amount, 10% is transferred to provincial governments and 90% to local governments. Local governments rely primarily on these transfers and have full discretion of their use (World Bank, 2006).
- The central government determines local taxes and rates. The local governments may create new local taxes, but they are subject to the central government approval (UCLG, 2007; UCLG 2010).

Key initiatives for participatory local governance

- In 1999, "Autonomy Laws" were passed that ushered in a new era of decentralization. Law No. 22/1999 gave districts more autonomy over public works, health, education and other duties (UCLG, 2007).
- In 2004, the "Autonomy Laws" were amended to allow for direct election of Bupati and mayors (UCLG, 2007).
- In 2009, a new law mandated subnational governments' authority over urban and rural property taxes for the continuation of decentralization policies over five years (UCLG, 2010).

Challenges for participatory local governance

- While decentralization has increased the responsibilities of local governments, tax revenues remain highly centralized and the own-source revenues of provincial and local governments only equal approximately 8% of revenue (UCLG, 2010).
- Decentralization has created "local egos" which may prove counterproductive when facing problems that require cooperation with other regions (UNESCAP, 2003).

List of sources:

Association of Indonesian Municipalities (APEKSI), 2014: http://apeksi.or.id/.

Indonesian Municipal Councils Association (ADEKSI), 2013: http://www.adeksi.or.id/.

Partnership for Democratic Local Governance in Southeast-Asia (DELGOSEA), 2014: "ADEKSI - Association of Indonesian Municipal Councils Indonesia."

Quota Project, 2014: "Indonesia."

Sautanama, 2011: http://sautanama.org.

The Partnership for Good Governance Refor (Kemitraan), 2014: http://www.kemitraan.or.id/.

UN Economic and Social Commission for Asia and the Pacific (UNESCAP), 2003: "Country Reports on Local Government Systems: Indonesia."

United Cities and Local Governments (UCLG), 2007: "UCLG Country Profiles: Indonesia."

United Cities and Local Governments (UCLG), 2010: "Local Government Finance: The Challenges of the 21st Century."

United Nations Development Program (UNDP), 2012: "International Human Development Indicators: Indonesia."

World Bank, 2002, Hofman B. and K. Kaiser: "Can Decentralization Help Rebuild Indonesia?"

World Bank, 2006, Shah, A.: "Public Sector Governance and Accountability Series: Local Governance in Developing Countries."

The Indonesia Governance Index (IGI)
Lenny Hidayat, Partnership for Governance Reform

Overview

The Indonesia Governance Index (IGI) is an assessment model that measures governance performance within four provincial arenas: political institutions, bureaucracy, civil society and economic society. The IGI has been effective at empowering citizens to hold local governments accountable based on publications of data and research findings.

IGI measures the functionality of local governance using a 4x6 grid framework that assesses the four provincial arenas against six good governance principles: participation, fairness, accountability, transparency, efficiency and effectiveness. In each cell there are indicators, which the IGI team justifies based on significance, relevance to governance processes, availability of data, discriminating power, and commonality across provinces. There are 89 indicators for the provincial level and 133 indicators for the district level.

IGI produces profiles of provinces that summarize governance performance by ranking areas of governance such as sub index gender, environment, and budget commitment for basic services and investment. Profiles also include statistical analysis of governance related issues and three types of qualified data: objective, perceptive and judgment. All scores are aggregated by calculating an index number from 1 to 10 for each indicator. Lower index scores indicate lower performances of individual functions per arena; a higher index score indicates better synergy and interaction between arenas.

Program participants

Since 2007, 102 researchers, nearly 20% of whom are women, and seven project management personnel have been involved in the making of IGI.

IGI engaged 1,857 well-informed persons (WIPs) of Indonesia from across the four provincial arenas. Approximately 10% were females.

Fifty experts compiled IGI's most recent Analytical Hierarchy Process which proposes a model for evaluating strong and weak e-government service delivery and ideal websites at the provincial and district levels.

Over an eight-year development process, more than 26,000 hours of data analysis have been carried out for the index.

Success factors

The IGI team learned that managing wide-scale research involves managing ethics, upholding procedure and securing commitment. It therefore designed a technical research protocol of in-depth training and intensive technical assistance for local researchers.

Evidence of success

As a proponent of transparency and accountability within Indonesia's local governments, IGI has received enormous, positive support and appreciation from various government officials, bureaucrats, civil society organizations, media, universities, governance experts, and economic society from national to local levels. It has shown how evidence-based policy making yields positive and productive changes in budgeting, paradigms, standards for governance impact, and interaction between governance actors.

Replication

UNDP's Oslo Governance Center (OGC) has used IGI as an example in their online governance portal. OGC also invited one of IGI's lead researchers to hold presentations for several African countries about establishing IGI, its strategy and lessons learned from data collection at conferences in Cairo, Egypt and Senegal. Additionally, this successful model has influenced several of Indonesia's local governments to assess effective research management and strategic planning using their own budget.

Addressing challenges

In response to difficult access and immediately unavailable data, the data collection period has been extended from three months to six months. IGI also utilizes its relationship with the media as a means to ensure successful dissemination of data and utilization of social media as a sharing platform.

Sustainability

IGI has increased the number of universities and institutes at both the national and local levels that conduct in-depth research. Though IGI is advocated by Indonesia's Ministry of Home Affairs, it is in the process of seeking additional funding because it cannot accept direct funding from the government.

References:

Indonesia Government Index (IGI), n.d.: www.kemitraan. or.id/igi

Indonesia Government Index (IGI), n.d.: "Frequently Asked Questions" http://www.kemitraan.or.id/igi/index. php/faq

"Analytical Hierarchy Process," 2013: http://www. igi-global.com/article/analytic-hierarchy-process-evaluation-government/76927

PLDI rank	47
Population	6,318,000
HDI rank	100/187
HDI score	0.700

Jordan has attempted political reforms to encourage participation and democratic behaviors as the government takes steps toward devolving its powers.

Local governance at a glance

- Jordan is divided into 12 governorates, 93 municipalities and the Greater Amman Municipality (EuropeAid, 2011).
- Governorates are headed by a King appointed governor. Municipalities are governed by an elected mayor and council (EuropeAid, 2011).
- Municipalities, supervised by the Ministry of Municipal Affairs, are not part of the central government and "not seen as local public entities with broader local responsibilities" (EuropeAid, 2011).
- Twenty five percent of municipal council seats are reserved for women (openDemocracy, 2013).

Civil society actors

- Partners-Jordan works to advance civil society and Jordan's social and political development by promoting mediation and conflict management and encouraging citizen participation (Partners-Jordan, 2014).
- The work of the Al-Hayat Center for Civil Society Development includes monitoring elections and the performance of elected councils, and promoting decentralization, local governance, civic education and women's empowerment (Al-Hayat Center, 2013).

Capacity building institutions

- The Jordan Institute of Public Administration (JIPA) provides technical training to build national and regional institutional capacity in the public sector through administrative and financial consultations (JIPA, 2010).
- The Visions Center for Strategic and Development Studies consults local municipalities on "institutional restructuring, public finance management approaches, local development issues and master planning" (Visions Center, 2014).

Fiscal control

- Municipalities have many sources of income: the central government, investment of municipality property, revenues or fees from municipal areas, fees from businesses in their jurisdiction, contributions from national and international institutions, and loans from development banks. However, their right to collect these taxes and fees is limited (EuropeAid, 2011; UCLG, 2007).

Key initiatives for participatory local governance

- In 1994, Jordan revised the 1955 Municipal Election Law to allow for mayors to be directly elected in all municipalities except Amman. The first nationwide municipal elections were then held in 1995 (NDI, 1995).
- In 2007, a new municipal law was enacted that reversed that of 2001 to reauthorize the election of council members and mayors (except in Amman). It also includes the quota for women in municipal councils (Carnegie, 2007).
- Currently, a law on a local governance and a newer municipal law have been drafted to "improve the representation and the authority of municipal and local councils" and "enhance citizens' participation in decision making" (The Jordan Times, 2014; Albawaba, 2014).

Challenges for participatory local governance

- Many municipalities face debt and lack resources, technical expertise, and transparency (UCLG, 2007).
- Although municipalities have begun conducting elections again, the central government has significant control to intervene at the local level (UCLG, 2007).
- The 2013 municipal election saw political parties boycotting, a very low voter turnout, vote-buying, and violence (Al-Monitor, 2013).
- Municipalities play a minor role; "municipal jurisdictions appear to cover only 3.6% of the whole territory (…), so there are significant territories under direct control of the State" (EuropeAid, 2011).

List of sources:

Albawaba, 2014: "A two way street? Jordanian government seeks public's feedback on 'reform drive'."

Al-Hayat Center for Civil Society Development, 2013: http://www.hayatcenter.org/index.php/en/.

Al-Monitor, 2013, Al-Samadi, T.: "Jordan's Local Elections See Low Turnout."

Carnegie Endowment for International Peace, 2007: "Arab Political Systems: Baseline Information and Reforms – Jordan."

EuropeAid, 2011: "The Quest for Decentralizing Government in the Hashemite Kingdom of Jordan: Some Preliminary Findings of a Situation Analysis."

Jordan Institute of Public Administration (JIPA), 2010: http://jipa.gov.jo/ar/index_en.shtml.

National Democratic Institute (NDI), 1995: "Democracy and Local Government in Jordan: 1995 Municipal Elections."

openDemocracy, 2013, Pietrobelli, M.: "The politics of women's rights promotion in Jordan."

Partners Jordan, 2014: http://www.partners-jordan.org/about.php.

The Jordan Times, 2014, Al Emam, D.: "New municipalities law aimed at entrenching decentralisation."

United Cities and Local Governments (UCLG), 2007: "UCLG Country Profiles: The Hashemite Kingdom of Jordan."

Visions Center for Strategic Development and Studies (Visions Center), 2014: http://jordanvisions.org/.

Decentralizing Jordan: Overcoming the "Middle East" Challenge
Ayoub Namour, Al-Hayat Center for Civil Society Development

Introduction

Democracy in the Middle East is not easy. Jordan, in particular, faces challenges, including the overwhelming influx of one million Syrian refugees to the already 6.5 million population. Yet, despite geographic and extreme geopolitical circumstances, Jordan maintains a secure internal environment for political pluralism that is a rare model for peaceful democratic transition in the Middle East.

Decentralization was introduced by King Abdullah II in 2011 to crystalize a participatory approach that systemically bridges the gap between the central government and local constituents. Two constitutional amendments were created: the Constitutional Court and the Independent Election Commission (IEC). This was widely perceived to reflect true commitment to democratization. A vigorous national debate over the future structure of local governance also ensued, resulting in two draft laws framing local democracy: the Municipalities' Law (which has been repeatedly amended to meet developmental needs), and the newly introduced Governorates' Councils Law.

The Jordanian government has referred the drafts to its Legislation and Opinion Bureau (LOB), for it to be legally edited and referred to the parliament to be discussed, approved and submitted to the King for royal approval to take effect. The process is expected to take until late 2014 - early 2015, and meanwhile public consultations are being held with CSOs, CBOs, municipal leaders and other stakeholders.

The Center Gives Up Some Power

Central government holds the lion's share of local authority, including budgeting, strategic planning, education, health, security, and most destructively, the power to dissolve any elected elected council at any time.

The impact of such domination is maximized by the fact the government is appointed by the King, not elected nor formed by the parliament. This results in local policies distant from local developmental needs and aspirations.

The government is now willing to deconcentrate its powers through a centrally supervised delegation of authorities. The new drafts introduce two councils for each of Jordan's 12 governorates: the Executive Council, a body appointed by the central government and the Governorate's Council, a body elected by local constituents.

Social Accountability

The structure has the potential for Jordan to sustain a gradual rate of democratic development while mitigating security concerns, and ultimately achieve a modern democratic model in the Middle East by the end of the next decade. Local governance shall be closer to people, and service quality should better meet citizen expectations, but this is conditioned on the executive's willingness to be held accountable.

There is a vital need for systematizing social accountability in legal paths that emphasize the participatory approach of local governance. Several CSOs have submitted recommendations that will potentially fill that gap, including: participatory budgeting, transparency portals, real-time tracking of local governments' performance and providing the right to vote local officials out of office.

Although Jordan was the first Arab country to introduce RTI, the current law does not sufficiently facilitate social accountability on the local level, and so will likely need to be amended.

Deepening Democracy

A major distortion of democracy in Jordan is the public perception of MPs as service providers - not legislators. This is highly attributable to the lack of local governance, which ideally should be in charge of providing local services. Thus, the newly introduced structure is expected to reform public awareness on the role of parliamentarians, and ultimately enhance parliamentary performance in legislation and oversight.

Now what?

Jordan is potentially the only Arab country to approach local democracy in an environment of stable security. But does Jordan have the financial and technical capacity to move on in developing the aimed participatory status? Public debt is approximately 75% of GDP and there are very few qualified local experts.

Thus, an international stand is required to fulfill the financial and technical demands of decentralization: not only for legislation and implementation strategies, but also for CSOs to raise public awareness and empower female leaders to create a gender-sensitive environment for women's participation.

KYRGYZSTAN

PLDI rank	28
Population	5,607,200
HDI rank	125/187
HDI score	0.622

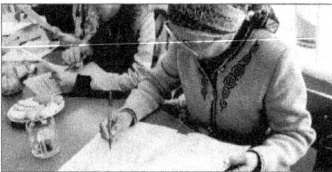

Kyrgyzstan's local governments have become more independent since the 2012 elections, but they still face problems of inefficiency and unprofessionalism (Freedom House, 2014).

Local governance at a glance
- Kyrgyzstan is divided into seven provinces (oblasts), 40 districts (rayons), two cities of national significance - Osh and Bishkek - and 23 of oblast and rayon significance, and 459 local communities (ayil okhomotus) (INTRAC, 2011).
- The oblast and rayon levels are part of the local state administration and are headed by an appointed governor, respectively Akim, and "receive executive constructions from the National level." Each ayil okhomotu has a representative body and executive organ that are accountable to the local population (INTRAC, 2011).
- Kyrgyzstan has no legislative gender quota at the subnational level (Quota Project, 2014).

Civil society actors
- The Coalition for Democracy and Civil Society, or "the Coalition," "promotes democracy, transparency and accountability of the government bodies" and "addresses other social issues through civic education, meetings and video conferences" (the Coalition, 2014).
- The Taza Shailoo Association strives to ensure free, transparent and fair elections and referendums in the country (Taza Shailoo, n.d.).

Capacity building institutions
- The Association of Municipalities of the Kyrgyz Republic (AMKP) was formed in 2006 to promote cooperation between municipalities and strengthen local governments (AMKP, 2012).
- The University of Central Asia (UCA) provides capacity building for civil servants to improve local self-government, or LSG (UCA, 2014).

Fiscal control
- Local authorities have the power to collect local taxes. However, the regional governments have had little freedom in negotiating shared tax rates with the central government (Moldogaziev, 2012).
- Locality-specific revenues are returned to their region of origin and additional national funds are transferred to lower levels of the government by a transparent formula (Moldogaziev, 2012).

Key initiatives for participatory local governance
- In 1991, various localities introduced their own taxes and fees and claimed responsibility for their budgets without direct accountability to the national government (Moldogaziev, 2012).
- In the late 1990s, a major accomplishment toward decentralization occurred when state-owned assets were smoothly transferred to rural municipalities (Freedom House, 2012).
- In 2001, the "Law on Local Self-government and Local State Administrations" was adopted. This regulates activities of local state power and local self-government organs. This law was re-drafted in 2011 "to make improvements to the issue of delineation of functions and responsibilities" (INTRAC, 2011) (UCLG, 2008).
- A 2008 law on local governance was established to ensure that local officials have financial and political resources necessary to meet the needs of the population (Freedom House, 2012).

Challenges for participatory local governance
- Though Kyrgyzstan has formally achieved its goals for decentralization, most local government officials lack professionalism and experience to govern according to new legislation (Freedom House, 2014).
- Representatives of local political parties lack experience with public service and bureaucracies, and local governments have little financial capacity to implement policy or respond to constituents' concerns (Freedom House, 2014).
- Ambiguity of the functions and power relations between organs of state and organs of local self-governments negatively affects the provision of services for the local population (INTRAC, 2011).

List of sources:
The Association of Municipalities (AMKP), 2012: http://www.citykr.kg/en/celi_i_zadachi.php.
Association "Taza Shailoo," n.d.: http://www.tazashailoo.kg/en/home.
Coalition for Democracy and Civil Society (the Coalition), 2014: www.linkedin.com/company/coalition-for-democracy-and-civil-society?trk=top_nav_home.
Freedom House, 2012: "Kyrgyzstan."
Freedom House, 2014: "Kyrgyzstan."
International NGO Training and Research Centre (INTRAC), 2011: "Decentralisation in Kyrgyzstan."
Moldogaziev, T., 2012, Eurasian Journal of Business and Economics: "Fiscal Decentralization and Revenue Stability in the Kyrgyz Republic, 1993-2010."
Quota Project, 2014: "Kyrgyzstan."
United Cities and Local Governments (UCLG), 2008: "UCLG Country Profiles: Central Asia."
University of Central Asia (UCA), 2014: http://www.ucentralasia.org/news.asp?Nid=659.

LEBANON

PLDI rank	45
Population	4,424,888
HDI rank	72/187
HDI score	0.745

The idea of decentralization was introduced in the 1989 Taif Accord, but it was not until 2014 that a bill for decentralization was drafted.

Local governance at a glance
- Lebanon is divided into six governorates, which are subdivided into districts, towns and villages. Municipalities, [administrative units below the district level], are the only form of administrative decentralization (UCLG, 2009).
- Municipal councils, elected by the municipality, elect their mayor. Villages and towns which are not a municipality elect a mukhtar (headman) and council of elders (UCLG 2009; Encyclopedia Britannica, 2014)
- The Ministry of Interior and Municipalities is responsible for municipalities and those villages not part of a municipality (UCLG, 2009).
- There are no legislative quotas for women at the subnational level (Quota Project, 2009).

Civil society actors
- The Lebanese Center for Policy Studies (LCPS) promotes transparency and accountable governance through advocacy, research and trainings. It focuses most specifically on judicial reforms, transparent budget processes, and decentralization and local governance (LCPS, 2014).
- The Lebanese Foundation for Permanent Civil Peace (LFCPC) encourages civic participation and stronger local government by working to increase the capacity of Lebanon's municipalities (LFCPC, 2005).

Capacity building institutions
- The Building Alliance for Local Advancement, Development, and Investment (BALADI) is a USAID program that encourages "municipalities (in cooperation with local NGOs, CSOs, and community members) to annually submit well-prepared and well-designed community projects for possible funding" (USAID, 2014).

Fiscal control
- Municipalities can only collect taxes on "rental rates, building permits, pipe maintenance, the use of municipal public land, advertisements in cinemas, cattle slaughtering, meeting rooms and certain types of businesses." These directly collected taxes make up 30% of the municipal budget (UCLG, 2009).
- According to the 1979 Law on Municipalities, the central government should collect certain taxes on behalf of municipalities and transfer some revenue directly back to them and to an Independent Municipal Fund. The central government began making these transfers only after 1997 (UCLG, 2009).

Key initiatives for participatory local governance
- Municipal elections were reinstated in 1998, leading to new impulse towards decentralization (LCPS, 2012).
- The formation of municipal unions across the country resulted in an emergence of important actors in support of the process toward decentralization (LCPS, 2012).
- In April 2014, the first bill to increase administrative decentralization was unveiled. It aimed to devolve more power and rights, including more financial autonomy and accountability for municipalities. The areas of infrastructure, health and transportation remain under the control of the central government (Zawya, 2014).

Challenges for participatory local governance
- "[I]n a society like Lebanon's with entrenched traditions of patronage, the danger is that decentralization simply shifts rather than eradicates the locus of corruption" (O'Sullivan, 2014).
- Sufficient administrative capacity for municipalities must be granted in order to enable them to cope with new tasks and responsibilities for more decentralization (O'Sullivan, 2014).
- Due to an implementation gap, the Independent Municipal Fund system "lacks transparency, thus breeding corruption and unfair distribution of resources. As a result, local municipalities often do not receive the full amounts allocated to them in the budget" (CIPE, 2014).

List of sources:
Center for International Private Enterprise (CIPE), 2014, Nakagaki, M.: "Can Decentralization Solve Political Gridlock in Lebanon?"
Encyclopedia Britannica, 2014: "Lebanon. Local Government."
Lebanese Center for Policy Studies (LCPS), 2012, Atallah, S., 2012: "Decentralization in Lebanon."
Lebanese Center for Policy Studies (LCPS), 2014: http://www.lcps-lebanon.org/about.php.
Lebanese Foundation for Permanent Civil Peace (LFCPC), 2005: http://www.kleudge.com/flpcp/projets_en.asp.
O'Sullivan, D., 2014, Executive Magazine: "Decentralization – the best way to tackle corruption?"
Quota Project, 2009: "Lebanon."
United Cities and Local Governments (UCLG), 2009: "UCLG Country Profiles: Lebanese Republic."
USAID, 2014: http://baladi-lebanon.org/.
Zawya, 2014: "Sleiman launches long-awaited bill to decentralize government."

Lebanon's Draft Decentralization Law Aims to Serve Development

Sami Atallah, Lebanese Center for Policy Studies

Although Lebanon's political system has managed to remain intact despite regional disasters – Gaza is destroyed, Syria is shattered, and Iraq is on the brink of collapse – the country faces at least two sets of challenges. The first is socio-economic: high youth unemployment, poor infrastructure, and weak public services, all of which are exacerbated by more than one million Syrian refugees currently in Lebanon. The second is the absence of an effective central government to address these challenges. With frequent deadlock in forming a government and electing a President and a Parliament, there is a strong incentive to decentralize public services to lower tiers of government so citizens do not remain hostage to political stalemates.

It is against this background that former President Suleiman launched a new Decentralization Law weeks before the end of his tenure. The draft law, to which I have contributed, was the work of a government appointed committee headed by Mr. Ziyad Baroud, a prominent lawyer, CSO activist, and decentralization advocate who also served as former Minister of Interior and Municipalities. The committee members included current and former government officials and advisors as well as independent experts.

In brief, the draft law transforms district leadership, known as "Qadas," from appointed positions into elected bodies. This is a monumental task since Qadas are integral to Lebanon's administrative framework and have a long history of representing the authority of the central government. The law endows these bodies with wide responsibilities to undertake developmental duties and equips them with fiscal resources through their own taxes and proper transfer systems.

Although it was part of the President's program when elected in May 2008, decentralization was put on the public agenda by CSOs as early as 1993. When Lebanon's national government failed to hold municipal elections, CSOs took up the cause. My organization, the Lebanese Center for Policy Studies (LCPS), was the first to take on the issue of decentralization by organizing a series of workshops that brought together academics, intellectuals, journalists, and civil society activists.

In 1997, the parliament approved the Prime Minister's draft law to extend the mandate of the country's municipal councils, which were last held in 1963. In response, the Lebanese Association for Democratic Elections (LADE), established largely by LCPS, was the first to press the government to hold municipal elections by organizing a national movement for local elections under the slogan "My Country, My Town, My Municipality." After

13 months of work, it managed to enlist more than 100 associations along with political party representatives, activists, and volunteers to collect more than 60,000 signatures. The campaign also mobilized the media of Lebanon and numerous Pparliament members. By June 14th, 1998, the government had held municipal elections in 600 out of 708 municipalities (the remaining municipalities were under Israeli occupation). More than 1.2 million Lebanese voters applied for election cards to exercise their constitutional right of suffrage, with 10,000 municipal council members joining the political class. Due to the success of this initiative, municipal elections are now held regularly every six years.

After the campaign for municipal elections, CSO work did not end. LCPS continued its policy work assessing municipal performance, evaluating bottlenecks and identifying problems in municipal transfers. These studies showed the importance of social accountability in the provision of services and the need to design transparent and equitable criteria for distribution, all of which have made it into the draft law. Moreover, the draft law provides for quota systems for women in both the Qada council and the executive authority, youth participation in the regional administrations, and transparency. The Qada must periodically collect, analyze and publish data that pertain to its performance, its audit report, and decisions that are public in nature. It gives citizens the right to access the decision of the executive authority so they can effectively monitor the work of the Qada.

PLDI rank	5
Population	4,190,435
HDI rank	174/187
HDI score	0.388

In 2011, Liberia approved a National Policy on Decentralization and Local Governance (NPDLG), which is the first meaningful decentralization policy after many unsuccessful attempts in the past (IREX, 2014).

Local governance at a glance

- Liberia is a unitary state divided into 15 counties. The counties are subdivided into 68 districts, districts into chiefdoms, chiefdoms into clans, and clans into towns or villages (VOLT, 2013).
- County authorities, city mayors, and township commissioners are appointed by the President (VOLT 2013).
- Liberia's Ministry of Internal Affairs (MIA) is responsible for overseeing local administration (MIA, 2014).
- Liberia has no gender quota provision or local level quotas (Quota Project, 2013).

Civil society actors

- Youth Partnership For Peace and Development (YPPD) seeks to increase youth participation in development and democracy in Liberia (YPPD, 2012).
- NAYMOTE empowers Liberia's community, especially youth leaders, to advocate for positive change at local levels (NAYMOTE, n.d.).
- The Liberia Women Media Action Committee (LIWOMAC) empowers "women in poor grassroots communities to fight off inequalities and participate in governance at the household, community and national levels" (LIWOMAC, 2014).

Capacity building institutions

- The Governance Commission (GC) drives decentralization and local governance policy. GC conducts research, consults Liberians on issues affecting governance, and recommends policy and institutional reforms to improve public service delivery at all levels of government (GC, n.d.).
- The Liberian Institute of Public Administration (LIPA) trains public officials on the function of government to improve democratic governance and the managerial capabilities of officials in all sectors and levels of the government (LIPA, n.d.).

Fiscal control

- The NPDLG "gives fiscal sharing power broadly to the local governments to allow them to control their own tax base and policies." Liberia's Legislature determines "the tax base for each county" and "prescribe(s) the types of taxes, rates, fees, and fines" levied by the local governments (IREX, 2010).
- "The bulk (of county authorities) expenditure management responsibilities are undertaken as agencies of central government, with no discretionary autonomy over allocations." (IMF, 2012).

Key initiatives for participatory local governance

- The Liberia Decentralisation and Local Development (LDLD) program started in 2007 to support the decentralization process and help local governments access development funds (UNCDF, 2013).
- The NPDLG, called for decentralization via the transfer of political, fiscal and administrative powers to local governments. This and ongoing governance reforms are yielding a more decentralized government (IBIS, 2012).
- In 2014, the Ministry of Finance prepared a plan to drive fiscal decentralization and capacity building forward (AllAfrica, 2014).
- The adoption of a new constitutional amendment by 2015 is expected to result in the enactment of a Local Government Act. Many hope it will foster decentralized and participatory local governance (DCID, 2014).

Challenges for participatory local governance

- Liberia has not held local elections since the end of the civil war in 2003. Those scheduled for 2008 were cancelled, ostensibly due to a lack of financial resources (Freedom House, 2011).
- Local governments lack institutional capacity, structured local administration and qualified staff, as well as a "system of clear, predictable and transparent financial transfers" (UCLG Africa and Cities Alliance, 2013).

List of sources:

AllAfrica, 2014: "Liberia: Finance Ministry Drives Fiscal Decentralization Plan."

Duke Center for International Development (DCID), 2014: "Liberian officials trained in fiscal decentralization."

Freedom House, 2011: "Liberia."

Governance Commission (GC), n.d.: www.goodgovernance.org.lr/overview.html.

IBIS, 2012: "Country Strategy for IBIS Liberia 2012 – 2016."

International Monetary Fund (IMF), 2012: "Liberia: Public Expenditure and Financial Accountability (PEFA) Assessment."

International Research & Exchange Board (IREX), 2010: "National Decentralization & Local Governance Policy."

Liberian Institute of Public Administration (LIPA), n.d.: www.lipa.gov.lr/public/.

Liberia Women Media Action Committee (LIWOMAC), 2014: http://www.gnwp.org/members/liwomac.

NAYMOTE, n.d.: www.naymote.com/what-we-do/.

Quota Project, 2013: "Liberia."

Republic of Liberia Ministry of Internal Affairs (MIA), 2014: "Liberia's Decentralization Secretariat Program."

UNCDF, 2013: "Liberia Decentralization and Local Development Programme. Final Report."

United Cities and Local Governments of Africa (UCLG Africa) and Cities Alliance, 2013: "Assessing the Institutional Environment of Local Governments in Africa."

Vision For Liberia Transformation (VOLT), 2013: "Politics."

Youth Partnership For Peace and Development (YPPD), 2012: www.yppdliberia.wordpress.com.

MALAWI

PLDI rank	9
Population	16,362,567
HDI rank	170/187
HDI score	0.418

Malawi's first local and multi party elections were held in 2000. However, the following local elections were delayed until May 2014 (CLGF, 2013; Freedom House, 2014).

Local governance at a glance
- The local government consists of four cities, 28 district councils, two municipal councils and one town council. All 35 local authorities are single tier (CLGF, 2013).
- Councilors each represent one ward and are elected for a five-year term (CLGF, 2013).
- The Ministry of Local Government and Community Development oversees the administration of local governments (CLGF, 2013).
- There are no gender quotas at the subnational level (Quota Project, 2013).

Civil society actors
- Youth Net and Counselling (YONECO) is committed to the empowerment of youth, women and children for the purpose of promoting human rights and democracy. Examples include counseling, civic education and networking services.
- SOS Démocratie aims to strengthen democracy by educating people about democratic principles, improving voter participation, and ensuring transparency and freedom of the voter's choice (SOS Démocratie, n.d.).

Capacity building institutions
- The National Local Government Finance Committee (NLGFC) furthers the fiscal decentralization by ensuring that local authorities have significant funds to carry out necessary projects (Chiweza, 2010).
- The Malawi Local Government Association (MALGA) lobbies on behalf of the local governments to promote the interests of the people (MALGA, n.d.).

Fiscal control
- The councils are responsible for collecting local taxes, but most of their revenue comes from the central government (CLGF, 2013).
- The Constitution provides for 5% of net government revenue to be transferred to local governments (CLGF, 2013).
- The National Local Government Finance Committee was created in 2001 to oversee the financial relationship between the central and local governments (Chiweza, 2010).

Key initiatives for participatory local governance
- In 1996, the Malawi Social Action Fund (MASAF) was launched to promote honest and effective governance and restructure fiscal responsibility to focus more heavily on local governments (World Bank, 2010).

- The Local Government Act of 1998 provided a framework for decentralization and established local councils (CLGF, 2013).
- In 1998, a new National Decentralization Policy (NDP) was approved. It "seeks to devolve powers and functions of governance and development to elected Local Government Units as reflected in the Constitution" (UNPAN, n.d.).
- In 2008, the second NDP was established. This NDP "seeks to provide a coherent framework for the implementation of decentralisation and also serves as a tool for coordinating donor support towards the decentralisation process" (Chiweza, 2010).

Challenges for participatory local governance
- Local elections were delayed until 2014. This suspension of local councils led to a "re-centralisation of political authority" (O'Neil and Cammack et al., 2014).
- There is a lack of accountability: local authorities are dysfunctional, service provision is failing and the political elite allow corruption (O'Neil and Cammack et al., 2014; O'Neil, 2014).
- Sector staff at the local level are appointed by Ministries and are thus accountable to the central government (O'Neil and Cammack et al., 2014).
- There are delays in Local Development Funds, a low capacity within councils to promote participation and development, and a lack of follow-up with projects (World Bank, 2010).

List of sources:
Chiweza, A., 2010: "A Review of the Malawi Decentralization Process: Lessons from Selected Districts."
Commonwealth Local Government Forum (CLGF), 2013: "Malawi."
Freedom House, 2014: "Malawi."
Malawi Local Government Association (MALGA), n.d.: http://www.malgamw.org/.
O'Neil, T., D. Cammack et al., 2014, ODI: "Fragmented governance and local service delivery in Malawi."
O'Neil, T., 2014, Open Democracy: "Will the new government and local councils improve delivery in Malawi?"
Quota Project, 2014: "Malawi."
United Nations Public Administration Network (UNPAN), n.d.: "Decentralisation Process in Malawi."
World Bank, 2010: "Social Development Notes: Demand for Good Governance."
Youth Net and Counselling (YONECO), 2014: http://www.yoneco.org/site/.

The Return of Councilors: Prospects and Challenges of Local Governance and Local Development in Malawi

Augustine Magolowondo, PhD., Netherlands Institute for Multiparty Democracy
(excerpted from a longer article available at localdemocracy.net)

The May 2014 elections were a unique opportunity for Malawi to reflect on the past and shape the future of its democracy. The elections coincided with Malawi's 50th year of independence and marked the return of elected District Councils. [Local elections should have been held in 2005, but were repeatedly delayed.]

Malawi's Decentralization Policy Framework is designed to give power to the people through elected representatives known as councilors. The absence of councilors in the local government system led traditional chiefs, politicians and officials to assume local authority roles without mechanisms to ensure transparency and accountability.

Local governments are to spearhead local development initiatives and facilitate local democratic participation. Councilors are responsible, as outlined by the Local Government Act (1998), for policy and promotion of local participatory democracy. The reintroduction of councilors raises local citizenry optimism for representation of their views and ideas. It is also expected to advance Malawi's local development agenda. However, a number of issues must be addressed.

1. Funding: Local authorities will succeed if they are adequately resourced. Presently, local authorities are financed through some local revenue, but mainly government grants. However, the central government's establishment of local development initiatives outside local government structures, - arguably to garner political leverage and entrench patronage - creates competition for funds. Transparency in funds allocation and aligning local initiatives with local government authorities is imperative.

2. Political will: Success in establishing a strong and consistent local government is dependent on the political will of the central government. The fact that local government is a constitutional requirement does not guarantee that the central government will implement it.

3. Clear roles: There are three areas of conflict: Members of Parliament (MPs), district executives and Traditional Leaders. The Local Government Amendment Act (2010) granted voting powers to MPs within the District Councils in their area, creating unbalanced power relations because MPs view councilors as juniors and competitors. District Commissioners or CEOs (in urban areas) are supposed to report to the Council, but are appointed by the central government. Lastly, in the period without local elections, traditional elders took on a greater governance role, leading now to conflicts.

4. Legal framework: Some of Malawi's recent legal amendments are expected to adversely affect councilors' effectiveness in local government. For example, mandating only two councilors per parliamentary constituency, when many are geographically and demographically large, reduces the capacity to bring government close to the people.

5. Capacity: Councilors often become spectators rather than main players. They need to have the competencies to fulfill their responsibilities. Capacity development will reduce over-extension of the central government and fill gaps hindering effective local governance.

6. Apathy: Malawi has not seen much interest among its people to participate in local government. There was a 14% voter turnout in the local elections of 2000. Additionally, women's participation could have been greater: women make up only 12.2% of elected councilors and 15.6% of elected Members of Parliament.

Conclusion

Section 147 of the Constitution states *"Local government authorities shall consist of local government officers who shall be elected... and the election shall be organized, conducted and supervised by the Electoral Commission."* Though this is again a reality for Malawi, the subsequent establishment of a strong and effective local government structure will be neither smooth nor immediate.

References

Chirwa, Wiseman Chijere, 2013, *Malawi Democracy and Political Participation.* AfriMAP and Open Society Initiative for Southern Africa.

United Nations Development Programme (UNDP), 1995, *Report on Decentralisation in Malawi: Local Governance and Development.* Lilongwe: GOM/UNDP.

PLDI rank	50
Population	29,239,927
HDI rank	64/187
HDI score	0.769

Malaysia currently has no elected local government. A traditional top-down approach to local administration constrains the capacity of local government and leads to a gap between demand and supply in its service delivery. However, growing community awareness is challenging the practice of centralized administration (Phang, 2008).

Local governance at a glance

- Malaysia is divided into 13 states (which are subdivided into districts) and three federal territories. The states are administered by the federal and state governments; the federal territories are directly administered by the federal government (MyGovernment, 2014).
- There are three tiers of government (federal, state, and local), and three types of local authorities (city, municipal, and district councils) that are responsible for providing basic infrastructure and public utilities. Municipalities and cities are also responsible for urban planning, public health and waste management. City councils engage in revenue collection and law enforcement (CLGF, 2013).
- The Ministry of Housing and Local Government (MHLG) executes and monitors all laws concerned with local government. In addition, the Ministry of Federal Territories and Urban Well-Being oversees local authorities in the federal territories of Kuala Lumpur, Putrajaya and Labuan (CLGF, 2013).
- Local elections in every state have been suspended indefinitely since 1965 under Section 15 of the Local Government Act 1976. Instead the state government appoints councilors for three-year terms in the local councils (CLGF, 2013).
- There are no legislated gender quotas at the local level (Chen, 2010).

Civil society actors

- Aliran Kesedaran Negara is Malaysia's oldest human rights group that advances social justice, democratic reforms - including transparency and accountability in governance - and citizen participation (Aliran, 2014).
- SUARAM is a human rights organization that promotes civil and political rights including freedom of expression, peaceful assembly, political accountability and democracy-building (SUARAM, 2014).

Capacity building institutions

- The National Institute of Public Administration (INTAN) provides training to public servants on financial, land and local government administration topics (INTAN, 2014).

Fiscal control

- Income for local authorities comes mainly from taxes, non-tax revenues, and allocations from federal and state governments (UCLG, 2006).
- "Self-assessed income tax" accounts for 60-70% of local authorities' revenue (CLGF, 2013).
- Launching grants, provided by the state to local authorities, need to be approved by MHLG. The amount of grants to a particular council depends on factors such as land area, population size, and expected revenue. The state governments have "direct financial authority" over local governments (UCLG, 2006).
- "Local government accounts for 1% of the GDP" (Phang, 2008).

Key initiatives for participatory local governance

- The Local Government Act 171 (1976) stipulated the appointment of councilors to local government from amongst members of the public. Act 172 stipulated local government's duty of taking into account representations and objections from the public (UCLG, 2006).
- In 1998, MHLG supported a national program to implement Local Agenda 21, a partnership program to expand community participation in the work of local government (Phang, 2008).
- In 2007, the central government started an electronic system, e-PBTs, to bring local government closer to citizens. The four elements of the system are accounts, taxation, e-submission, and complaints (CLGF, 2013).

Challenges for participatory local governance

- Autonomy and capacity of the local government are constrained by the central government's delegation of additional burdensome services that tax their financial and human resources. One example is local government's responsibility to address the rise in urban crime rates (Phang, 2008).
- The central government's tight control of the local government strains autonomy and public participation at the local level (Phang, 2008).

List of sources:

Commonwealth Local Government Forum (CLGF), 2013: "Country profile: Malaysia."

Chen, L., 2010, European Journal of Comparative Economic Studies: "Do Gender Quotas Influence Women's Representation and Policies?"

MyGovernment: The Government of Malaysia's Official Portal, 2014: "Subdivisions."

National Institute of Public Administration, 2014: http://www.intanbk.intan.my/i-portal/.

Persatuan Aliran Kesedaran Negara, 2014: http://aliran.com/.

Phang, S., 2008, Commonwealth Journal of Local Government: "Decentralization or Recentralization? Trends in local government in Malaysia."

Suara Rakyat Malaysia (SUARAM), 2014: http://www.suaram.net/.

United Cities and Local Governments (UCLG), 2006: "Malaysia."

MALI

PLDI rank	6
Population	14,853,572
HDI rank	182/187
HDI score	0.344

Mali has a long history of progress toward decentralization. However, there remains obstacles to fulfilling the goal of consolidating the democratization process and attaining sustainable development carried out by local actors (IMF, 2013)

Local governance at a glance

- The country is divided into eight Regions and the capital district called Bamako, which are divided into 49 cercles (districts). Cercles are subdivided into 703 municipalities (TSEP, 2014).
- Each municipality has municipal councils whose councilors are elected for five-year terms by citizens of the municipality. The councilors then elect a mayor (TSEP, 2014).
- The Ministry of Territorial Administration, Decentralization and Regional Planning (MATDAT) oversees the local sectors of governance.
- Mali has no legislated gender quota at the national or sub-national level (Quota Project, 2014).

Civil society actors

- SOS Démocratie works to ensure fair elections with increased citizen turnout (SOS Démocratie, 2013).
- Groupe Pivot Droits et Citoyenneté des Femmes au Mali (GP/DCF) works to reach gender equality in families, end violence against women, and strengthen women's citizenship and participation in power (GP/DCF, n.d.).
- The Forum of Civil Society Organizations (FOSC) provides a space for dialogue and participation to strengthen democracy and sustainable development (FOSC, 2011).

Capacity building institutions

- The Support Program for Local Authorities (PACT) works under MATDAT to strengthen the capacity of local governments and ensure that local authorities are effectively carrying out responsibilities (PACT, 2013).
- The Association of Municipalities of Mali (AMM) includes all municipalities and promotes the decentralization and deepening of local democracy (AMM, 2014).

Fiscal control

- The budget of local governments is composed of "(i) local tax revenues collected with the help of the tax authorities; (ii) government budget transfers (solidarity subsidies to make up for regional disparities); and (iii) investment grants (...) through the National Local Government Investment Agency" (World Bank, 2010).
- Transfers from the central government are set on an ad hoc basis (UCLG Africa and Cities Alliance, 2013).

Key initiatives for participatory local governance

- While the 1992 Constitution provided the principles for decentralization, the 1993 law set the framework. It established regions, cercles and municipalities, and constituted elected councils (WRI and Landesa, 2011).
- The 1996 Principal Decentralization Law shifted responsibilities for protecting natural resources and managing lands to local government (WRI and Landesa, 2011).
- In 2002, the National Government signed decrees to transfer responsibilities concerning health, education and water to local authorities (SNV and CEDELO, 2004).
- The 2005 National Decentralization Policy Framework Paper (2005-2014) focuses on "capacity building in territorial communities, improvement of devolution, development of citizenship and development of private service delivery at the local level" (PD, 2011).

Challenges for participatory local governance

- The local government faces several challenges: establishing competence at the local level has been accompanied by insufficient resources, weak resource-mobilization leads to dependency on transfers from the central government, lack of budget decentralization, and insufficient representation of civil society (World Bank, 2013).
- Financial transfers from the central government are unpredictable and conditional, and thus impede local autonomy (UCLG Africa and Cities Alliance, 2013).

List of sources:

Association of Municipalities of Mali (AMM), 2014: http://www.coopdec-mali.org.

Evaluation of the Paris Declaration (PD), 2011: "Country Evaluation Mali. Executive Summary."

Forum of Civil Society Organizations (FOSC), 2011: www.societecivilemali.org.

Groupe Pivot Droits et Citoyenneté des Femmes au Mali (GP/DCF), n.d.: http://www.jeunesse.francophonie.org/annuaire/societe-civile/groupe-pivot-droits-et-citoyennete-des-femmes-au-mali.

International Monetary Fund (IMF), 2013: "Mali: Poverty Reduction Strategy Paper."

Quota Project, 2014: "Mali."

SNV and CDELO, 2004: "Decentralisation in Mali: Putting Policy into Practice."

SOS Démocratie, 2013: http://sosdemocratiemali.org.

Support Program for Local Authorities (PACT), 2013: http://www.pact-mali.org.

Trans-Saharan Elections Project (TSEP), 2014, University of Florida: "The Electoral System. Mali."

United Cities and Local Governments of Africa (UCLG Africa) and Cities Alliance, 2013: "Assessing the Institutional Environment of Local Governments in Africa."

World Bank, 2010: "Mali Public Expenditure Management and Financial Accountability Review."

World Bank, 2013: "Implementation Status & Results. Mali. ML-Governance and Budget Decentralization Technical Assistance Project (P112821)."

World Resources Institute (WRI) and Landesa, 2011: "The Challenge of Decentralization in Mali."

MAURITIUS

PLDI rank	37
Population	1,291,456
HDI rank	80/187
HDI score	0.737

Mauritius is a constitutional republic with a decentralized system of government structures that govern the country's small island dependencies, including Rodrigues Island, which has its own government (CLGF, 2013).

Local governance at a glance

- Mauritius has three tiers of government: central, local, and village government. There is no constitutional provision for local government other than the Rodrigues Regional Assembly (CLGF, 2013).
- The local government in Mauritius has two tiers: urban councils (municipalities) and rural authorities (district councils), which oversee village councils. Currently, there are five municipal councils across seven geographical areas. In the rural areas, there is a two-tier system: seven district councils and 130 village councils (CLGF, 2013).
- The Ministry of Local Government and Outer Islands (MLGOI) is responsible for overseeing local authorities (CLGF, 2013).
- The 2011 Local Government Act (LGA) mandates that municipal council and village council elections be held every six years. District councilors are elected indirectly by secret ballots from members of village councils (CLGF, 2013).
- The 2011 LGA states that "a list of reserve candidates for the election of municipal city councilors, municipal town councilors or village councilors, for any vacancy which may occur between two elections, shall not comprise more than two-thirds of persons of the same sex and not more than two consecutive candidates on the list shall be of the same sex" (Quota Project, 2014).
- Village councils are required to hold monthly meetings for general business. They have a part-time chair who is elected every two years in a secret ballot by the village councilors (CLGF, 2013).

Civil society actors

- The Allied Network for Policy, Research & Actions for Sustainability (ANPRAS) promotes sustainable living at the grassroots level through community driven actions and encourages policy research and academic publications (ANPRAS, 2013).
- The Mauritius Council of Social Service (MACOSS) is an umbrella organization for NGOs that promotes social and community development and voluntary actions (MACOSS, 2012).

Capacity building institutions

- There are currently two local government associations in Mauritius that unite local governments on various issues: the Association of Urban Authorities and the Association of District Councils (CLGF, 2013).

- The Ministry of Local Government and Outer Islands (MLGOI) works to empower and provide appropriate support to local authorities to enable them to manage the affairs of the local communities effectively and efficiently (MLGOI, n.d.).

Fiscal control

- Municipal and district councils are empowered to raise revenue through the following fees: building and land use permits, trade, markets, cemeteries, scavenging, traffic violations and advertisements. Municipal councils can also raise revenue through a general property rate (CLGF, 2013).
- The annual 'grant in aid' for all local authorities is voted in at the beginning of the financial year as part of the MLGOI budget. It is distributed in monthly installments to each local authority (CLGF, 2013).

Key initiatives for participatory local governance

- The 2011 LGA provides for formal consultation processes with civil society on local governance issues (CLGF, 2013).
- In 2012, the government - in collaboration with local authorities - launched an e-government portal allowing members of the public to access information, make applications and inquiries, and file complaints (CLGF, 2013).

Challenges for participatory local governance

- The political representation and participation of women remains low despite legal provisions. Attitudes preventing women's participation remain unchanged (Bunwaree and Kasenally, 2005).
- Despite the relatively decentralized fiscal control system, financial estimates for local authorities must be approved by the MLGOI. The MLGOI must also approve the annulment of bad debts and disbursement, withdrawal and reallocation of funds. Annulling bad debts also requires the approval of the minister (CLGF, 2013).

List of sources:

Allied Network for Policy, Research & Actions for Sustainability (ANPRAS), 2013: http://www.anpras.org/

Bunwaree, S. and R. Kasenally, 2005: "Political Parties and Democracy in Mauritius".

Commonwealth Local Government Forum (CLGF), 2013: "Country Profile: Mauritius."

Mauritius Council of Social Service (MACOSS), 2012: http://www.macoss.intnet.mu/.

Ministry of Local Government and Outer Islands (MLGOI), n.d.: http://localgovernment.gov.mu/English/AboutUs/Pages/Mission-and-Vision.aspx.

Quota Project, 2014: "Mauritius.

PLDI rank	40
Population	120,847,477
HDI rank	61/187
HDI score	0.775

Since the early 2000's, Mexico has created multiple programs to spearhead decentralization: coordination of rural development, creating institutional platforms, and appropriately portioning funds (World Bank, 2006).

Local governance at a glance

- Mexico has 31 States and one Federal District (Mexico City). States are divided into 2,477 municipalities governed by Municipal Councils (Ayuntamiento) and headed by a mayor (SudHistoria, 2011).
- In Oaxaca, 412 municipalities have traditional, indigenous leadership selection and community assemblies. Since 2005, only 12% of municipalities used secret ballots (AU, 2005).
- The Secretary of Governance is responsible for local government (SEGOB, 2012).
- Gender quotas are regulated by each state. Article 41 of the Federal Constitution requires that political parties create rules to ensure gender equality on electoral lists (Quota Project, 2014).

Civil society actors

- The Latin American and Caribbean Network for Democracy (REDLAD) acts as a platform to share information, best practices and strategies regarding democracy and human rights in the region (REDLAD, 2014).
- Observatorio Ciudadano is a platform that welcomes constructive criticism to solve problems and influence public policy in Oaxaca (Observatorio Ciudadano, n.d.).

Capacity building institutions

- The Secretariat of Agriculture, Livestock, Rural Development, Fisheries and Food (SAGARPA) is a program that has made advances in the decentralization of Mexico's rural development program (World Bank, 2006).
- The Association of Local Authorities of Mexico (AALMAC) is a civil association that acts as a forum for municipalities and promotes the training of authorities and officials (AALMAC, 2011).

Fiscal Control

- Most rural development funds come from federal sources. State governments have small influence on the allocation of these funds (World Bank, 2006).
- Local governments are assigned urban property and car registration taxes, but are not allowed to implement their own tax system (UCLG, 2010).
- Local government expenditures account for 6.5% of total government expenditure, which is 2% of GDP (UCLG, 2010).

Key initiatives

- The 2001 Ley de Desarrollo Rural Sustentable (LDRS) advanced decentralization by creating institutional platforms. LDRS also mandates the signing of agreements between federal secretariats and the states to implement sectoral programs (World Bank, 2006).
- In June 2002, legislation was issued mandating the preparation of a Programa Especial Concurrente (PEC) to coordinate rural development actions of relevant secretariats (World Bank, 2006).

Challenges for participatory local governance

- There is limited participation by civil society and a need for citizen education on government because information is not readily available [online] (World Bank, 2007).
- Subnational governments are weak in their strategic planning, procurement, financial management, collection of locally raised revenues, capacities to develop investment projects, monitoring, and dissemination of outcomes (IDB, 2010).
- In the absence of civil service, new municipal mayors bring in new administrative staff, making it difficult to establish lasting programs (Sisk et al, 2001).
- Some municipal governments lack basic capacities, such as police forces, and the ability to govern effectively (Bertelsmann Stiftung, 2014).

List of sources:
American University Department of Government (AU), 2005: "Elections by Customary Law in Oaxaca, Mexico."
Association of Local Authorities of Mexico (AALMAC), 2011: http://www.aalmac.org.mx/.
Bertelsmann Stiftung, 2014: "Sustainable Government Indicators (SGI). 2014 Mexico Report."
InterAmerican Development Bank (IDB), 2010: "Mexico."
The Latin American and Caribbean Network for Democracy (REDLAD), 2014: http://www.redlad.org/
Observatorio Ciudadano, n.d.: http://www.conseguridadoaxaca.org/menu.html
Quota Project, 2014: "Mexico."
Secretariat of Agriculture, Livestock, Rural Development, Fisheries and Food (SAGARPA), 2013: http://www.sagarpa.gob.mx/Paginas/default.aspx.
Secretary of Governance (SEGOB), 2012: http://www.paraosc.segob.gob.mx/es/PARAOSC/home.
Sisk, T., 2001: "Democracy at the Local Level."
SudHistoria, 2011: "Corruption, Decentralisation and Caciquismo in Mexico in the last decade."
United Cities and Local Governments (UCLG), 2010: "Local Government Finance: The Challenges of the 21st Century."
World Bank, 2006: "Mexico: Decentralization of Rural Development Programs."
World Bank, 2007: "The Federal Procurement System: Challenges and Opportunities."

PLDI rank	13
Population	32,521,143
HDI rank	130/187
HDI score	0.591

In 2011, Morocco voted in favour of a new constitution stating that "territorial organization of the kingdom is decentralized" and "founded on an advanced regionalization" (IDEA, 2012). However, the issue of decentralization has not always gotten much attention and therefore the progress is still slow (Ottaway, 2013).

Local governance at a glance

- The local government structure comprises 16 regions divided into provinces and prefectures, and then urban or rural communes (Rao and Chakraborty, 2006).
- Regions are administered by a Wali (governor), appointed by the King, and a regional council, elected by direct universal suffrage. Provinces are governed by local government authorities, appointed by the King, and an assembly, elected by municipal councils. Communes have an elected mayor and a municipal council (GlobalSecurity, 2011).
- The Ministry of the Interior and the Ministry of Finance are responsible for the administration and supervision of local governments (UCLG, 2008).
- Morocco has a 12% quota of women at communal elections. In regional councils, a minimum of one third of seats are held for women (Quota Project, 2014).

Civil society actors

- By using a participatory development approach, the High Atlas Foundation (HAF) empowers rural and disadvantaged communities, fosters partnerships, and offers training to support grassroots initiatives and promote development (HAF, 2014).
- The Center for Humanities Studies and Research (MADA) educates youth, promotes democratic values and dialogue between young people, and strengthens cooperations between local institutions, both public and private (MADA, n.d).

Capacity building institutions

- The National Association of Local Governments of Morocco (ANCLM) promotes decentralization through its more than 1,600 members, providing them with legal assistance and training (ANCLM, n.d.).

Fiscal control

- Local governments produce their own revenue, but also receive funds from the central government's collected taxes and extra-budgetary resources such as loans (Rao and Chakraborty, 2006).
- Local authorities can legally raise charges and taxes, but do not have fiscal control over setting taxes or deciding on taxable bases or rates. The central government holds responsibility for taxation and budgeting at all levels of administration (UCLG, 2008; GlobalSecurity, 2011).

Key initiatives for participatory local governance

- The first step towards decentralization occurred in 1997 when the country was divided into 16 regions (Ottaway, 2013).
- In 2000, a new Municipal Charter was adopted. It included the possibility for communes to create partnerships with NGOs and the extension of municipal councils' responsibilities and powers (UCLG, 2008).
- The 2005 National Initiative for Human Development promoted new participatory local governance mechanisms to empower communities and improve accountability and transparency in decision-making processes at the local level (Bergh, 2010).
- The 2011 Constitution "establish[es] a constitutional monarchy with separation of powers" and "enhanced responsibilities for local and regional governments" (Moroccan American Center, 2011).

Challenges for participatory local governance

- Prefectures and provinces have limited power, almost no budgetary autonomy, and are tightly controlled by the central government. Thus, real decentralization is still not established (IDEA, 2012).
- The central government is strongly represented on the local level as regional Walis are appointed rather than elected (IDEA, 2012).
- Regionalization and decentralization, as stated by the new Constitution, must result in more than a shift of responsibilities. This should be accompanied by strong capacity-building efforts on the local level (AbiNader, 2013).

List of sources:

AbiNader, J., 2013, IdeaCom: "Morocco's CESE Project: Regionalization empowering local populations."

Bergh, S., 2010, Journal Economic and Social Research: "Assessing Local Governance Innovations in Morocco in Light of the Participatory Budgeting Experience in Brazil."

Center for Humanities Studies and Research (MADA), n.d.: http://centremada.over-blog.com.

GlobalSecurity.org, 2011: "Morocco Government."

High Atlas Foundation, 2014: http://www.highatlasfoundation.org.

International Institute for Democracy and Electoral Assistance (IDEA), 2012, Madani, M., D. Maghraoui and S. Zerhouni: "The 2011 Moroccan Constitution: A Critical Analysis."

Moroccan American Center, 2011: "FAQ: Reforms in Morocco."

National Association of Local Governments of Morocco (ANCLM), n.d.: http://anclm.ma.

Ottaway, M., 2013: "Morocco: 'Advanced Decentralization' Meets the Sahara Autonomy Initiative."

Quota Project, 2014: "Morocco."

Rao, G. and L. Chakraborty, 2006: "Fiscal Decentralization and Local Level Gender Responsive Budgeting in Morocco."

United Cities and Local Governments (UCLG), 2008: "UCLG Country Profiles: Kingdom of Morocco."

The Process of Decentralization in Morocco: Leisurely but Progressive

Prof. Mokhtar Benabdallaoui, University in Casablanca

The first local elections in Morocco were organized on May 29, 1960, a few months after independence. This is a strong sign of the importance given to the issue of decentralization at a very early time.

However, that did not mean that the state was committed to democracy. Decentralization was partly destined to promote local elites - the privileged allies of the regime. It was also handicapped by a strong dose of concentration of power in the central government.

Local and legislative elections were organized on a regular basis since that day, but with many failures, such as fraud, political interference and corruption.

A first project on regionalization was announced in 1971. It had economic objectives, designed to lighten regional disparities. Participatory democracy wasn't on the agenda.

In the constitution of 1996 a decisive step was taken: Article 100 stipulated, for the first time, that regions are official land areas. This allows regions to acquire legal personality and financial autonomy.

Regionalization in Morocco is not only related to economic or administrative reform; it is also presented as a definitive solution to the Western Sahara conflict: a compromise between Morocco's annexation and the independence claimed by separatists.

After the Constitution of 1996, a law on regions was passed in 1997. A new mission was attributed to the regions: they become a platform for a dialogue between the population and the administration. Representatives were elected indirectly among local districts, there was no real representation of the population, and the terms of reference on management were very general. The main restriction was the prerogatives of the governor as the only one authorized to sign financial documents; no budget could be spent without his agreement.

The latest Constitution, in 2011, gives a qualitative transformation to decentralization. It dedicates Chapter 9 to an issue, titled: "Regions & Districts." It is composed of 11 articles from 135 to 146. These articles stipulate that districts should be a subject of public law and managed democratically, with the values of cooperation and solidarity. They guarantee citizen participation in the management of affairs and enhance participation in integrated and sustainable human development. The prerogatives are now very large and allow us to talk about democratic participation.

The 2011 Constitution required a new law of regions, which is what a recent draft law on June 26, 2014 intends to accomplish. This new draft consolidates all aspects of the former law, and adds many new features. The region is now defined as a district: a subject of public law, with a legal personality, and administrative and financial independence. The government recognizes that the region has the authority to execute deliberation and decisions, and is thus considered the privileged partner of the state.

This last draft brought three major innovations: (1) the regional council will be elected by direct suffrage as a means to consolidate its legitimacy; (2) the governor will no longer be in charge of the budget, rather the president of the council - as head of executive authority in the region - will absolve that power; and (3) the council will create two advisory bodies, with business people, civil society and NGOs able to present petitions to the regional council.

This new turn of events permits us to be very optimistic and believe that decentralization and participatory democracy are progressing. However, two issues are still under question: the limit of the prerogative of the governor, and whether this proposal will be implemented in the Western Sahara as a last offer to the separatists or as a foretaste for a more rigorous autonomy.

NEPAL

PLDI rank	28
Population	27,474,377
HDI rank	157/187
HDI score	0.463

Local government in Nepal is a challenge. The country is still largely centralized and there have been no elected local governments since 2002 (GDI, 2013; World Bank, 2014).

Local governance at a glance
- The local government is divided into a middle tier of 75 districts, each with a District Development Committee (DDC). Districts are sub-divided into 58 municipalities and 3,913 Village Development Committees (VDCs). VDCs are divided into wards and serve as the lowest level of service delivery in the system (GDI, 2013; World Bank, 2014).
- Municipalities and VDCs are directly elected and the head of administration is appointed by the Ministry of Federal Affairs and Local Development, which oversees all local bodies (MoFALD) (UCLG, 2007; World Bank, 2014).
- Forty Percent of nominated candidates for municipal council elections must be women (Quota Project, 2014).

Civil society actors
- At the district level, the GoGo Foundation has a network of Good Governance Clubs that advocate for accountable, transparent, and participatory governance (GoGo Foundation, 2014).

Capacity building institutions
- The Local Governance and Community Development Programme (LGCDP) aims to improve local governments' capacity for service delivery, accountability and human resources (LGCDP, 2014).
- It also works toward alleviating poverty through community-lead participatory development, and the creation of inclusive, accountable and responsive local governments (GDI, 2013).
- The Local Governance and Accountability Facility (LGAF) is a national program that fosters citizen engagement and develops the capacity of marginalized groups and civic organizations to improve transparency and accountability in local government (LGAF, 2014).

Fiscal control
- Municipalities receive grants and revenues collected by the central government. They can also tax for housing, land, rent, enterprises, vehicles, properties, entertainment, and impose service charges and fees (UCLG, 2007).
- DDCs receive budgetary transfers from the central government, can impose fees and service charges, and tax transportation routes and certain goods (UCLG, 2007).
- VDCs can tax housing, land, rent, markets, vehicles, businesses, and natural resources; they can also impose service charges and fees (UCLG, 2007).

Key initiatives for participatory local democracy
- The Decentralization Act of 1982 devolved responsibilities to the district level government (UCLG, 2007).
- After democracy was restored in 1991, three acts furthered decentralization reforms in 1992: the District Development Committee Act, the Village Development Committee Act, and the Municipality Act (UCLG, 2007).
- The Local Self Governance Act (LSGA) of 1999 allocated significant responsibilities in service delivery and mandated partial autonomy to local bodies for decision-making and participation (UCLG, 2007).
- By February 2015, Nepal aims to promulgate its new constitution (Ranjitkar, 2104), which will include "a clarification of the roles and responsibilities for the tiers of local government, provisions for a more secure base for local elected officials," and more transparent and formula-based fund transfers (UCLG, 2010).

Challenges for participatory local democracy
- There have been no local elections since 2002. Instead, local governments are administered by interim, unelected bodies run by appointed bureaucrats (GDI, 2013).
- Corruption is rampant in local government bodies and seriously affects the local governments' ability to perform necessary services, resulting in the loss of legitimacy from the perspective of Nepali citizens (GDI, 2013).
- Although LSGA was considered a milestone, its major elements have not been implemented, local government funding is very low and revenue collection is limited due to larger municipalities (UCLG, 2007; World Bank, 2014).

List of sources:

German Development Institute (GDI), 2013, Mallik, V.: "Local and community governance for peace and development in Nepal."

Good Governance (GoGo) Foundation, 2013: http://www.gogofoundation.org/.

Local Governance Accountability Facility (LGAF), 2014: http://www.lgaf.gov.np/.

Local Governance and Community Development Programme (LGCDP), 2014: http://www.lgcdp.gov.np/home/index.php.

Quota Project, 2014: "Nepal."

Ranjitkar, S., 2014, Scoop. Independent News: "Nepal: Promulgating A New Constitution By February 2015."

United Cities and Local Governments (UCLG), 2007: "UCLG Country Profiles: Federal Democratic Republic of Nepal."

United Cities and Local Governments (UCLG), 2010: "Local Government Finance: The Challenges of the 21st Century."

World Bank, 2014, Farvacque-Vitkovic, C. and M. Kopanyi: "Municipal Finances. A Handbook for Local Governments."

PLDI rank	16
Population	17,831,270
HDI rank	186/187
HDI score	0.304

Niger suffered significant political and institutional instability, including military coups, in 1996, 1999, and 2010. Niger responded with the 2010 Constitution which established an institutional architecture for a republic consisting of bodies and frameworks for cooperation on issues of national interest (IMF, 2013).

Local governance at a glance

- Niger has three levels of subnational government: eight regions, 36 departments, and 265 municipalities, which make up the only functioning level of local authority. The regions and departments are led by councils and council leaders. The municipalities are led by councils and mayors (UCLG, 2008).
- Niamey, Maradi, Tahoua, and Zinder are urban communities with councils composed of delegates from each member municipality. Urban community council leaders are elected by the delegates (UCLG, 2008).
- "State representatives have control over the a posteriori legality of the actions of municipal authorities" (UCLG, 2008).
- There are gender quotas at the subnational level. "In parliamentary and local elections, the lists submitted...should include candidates of both sexes. ...(T)he proportion of elected candidates of either sex, should not be less than 10%. (Quota Project, 2014)."

Civil society actors

- The Association des Femmes Juristes du Niger (AFJN) works to improve the legal status of women (GNB, 2014).
- The Association Nigérienne de Défense des Droits de l'homme (ANDDH) provides training and civic education on human rights (ANDDH, 2012).

Capacity building institutions

- The Association des Municipalités du Niger (AMN) seeks to promote sustainable development by strengthening capacities of municipalities (AMN, 2011).

Fiscal control

- Local authorities send their financial and administrative accounts to the State Audit Office for review at the end of each fiscal year (UCLG, 2008).
- Municipalities are primarily funded by central government allocations and tax revenue. Local and state authorities also have shared taxes (UCLG, 2008).
- Local councils have authority to create remunerative duties that pay for services beneficial to the taxpayer. These must be delivered by the region, department, or municipality. Councils can also add tax surcharges to the central government's taxes and surcharges (UCLG, 2008).

Key initiatives for participatory local governance

- In 1964, Niger adopted Law No. 64/023, which created administrative constituencies and included local authorities in the framework of state centralization (UCLG, 2008).
- Developed in 2000, the Poverty Reduction Strategy Document called for "the promotion of good governance, strengthening human and institutional capacity and decentralization" to achieve stronger and sustainable political, economic, and local governance (UCLG, 2008).
- The High Commission for Modernization of the State created the National Policy on Modernization of the State, designed to increase the quality and accessibility of government services provided to citizens (IMF, 2013).
- The National Decentralization Policy of March 2012 gave the local government control over the implementation of policies, good governance, sustainable local development, and local democracy (IMF, 2013).

Challenges for participatory local governance

- Local governments are limited by the inability to mobilize internal resources to fulfill responsibilities and service delivery (IMF, 2013).
- The illiteracy level and lack of training and capacity of the large number of councilors has resulted in weak local authority bodies with reduced autonomy (UCLG, 2008).
- Decentralization and the 2004 creation of elected municipal authorities have been carried out without solid political support (de Sardan, 2012).

List of sources:

Association des Municipalités du Niger (AMN), 2011: https://www.facebook.com/pages/AMN-Association-des-Municipalit%C3%A9s-du-Niger/208759179173618?sk=info.

Association Nigérienne de Défense des Droits de l'homme (ANDDH), 2012: http://anddh-niger.org/.

Girls Not Brides (GNB), 2014: http://www.girlsnotbrides.org/members/association-des-femmes-juristes-du-niger-afjn/.

International Monetary Fund (IMF), 2013: "Niger: Poverty Reduction Strategy Paper."

de Sardan, J., 2012: "Providing public goods: Local responses to policy incoherence and state failure in Niger."

Quota Project, 2014: "Niger."

United Cities and Local Governments (UCLG), 2008: "Country Profile: Niger."

NIGERIA

PLDI rank	25
Population	168,833,776
HDI rank	153/187
HDI score	0.471

Nigeria is one of the most decentralized countries in Africa. However, local governments face difficulties delivering social and economic services due to a "mismatch between local government revenue powers and their expenditure responsibilities" (IFPRI, 2009).

Local governance at a glance

- Nigeria is divided into 36 states and the Federal Capital Territory of Abuja. The states compromise 768 local government authorities and six area councils of Abuja (CLGF, 2013).
- Local councils are directly elected and consist of 10 to 13 councilors (CLGF, 2013).
- The Ministry of Local Government is responsible for developing and maintaining responsive local government, managing budget proposals and promoting capacity building initiatives (Ministry of Local Government, 2013).
- Nigeria does not have legislated gender quotas (British Council, 2012).

Fiscal control

- Taxes are raised and collected by the federal and state governments. The local governments are able to collect some local taxes (i.e. haulage, hawking, and markets) and they receive funding from the state government and a federal account allocation (CLGF, 2013).
- States and local governments control approximately 50% of the government's total revenues; approximately 20% is allocated for local governments (CLGF 2013).

Civil society actors

- The Centre for Democracy and Development (CDD) strengthens democratic development and focuses on capacity-building, policy advocacy, and democratic governance (CDD, 2014).
- The Center for Environment, Human Rights and Development (CEHRD) educates rural communities about their rights and empowers them via education and assistance (CEHRD, 2012).
- The Female Leadership Forum (FLF) supports women leaders and enhances the participation of youth on the local and national level (FLF, 2012).

Capacity building institutions

- The Association of Local Governments of Nigeria (ALGON) represents all local governments and provides them with services and support to ensure that participatory development approaches are adopted in urban and rural local government areas for effective local development (CLGF, 2013).
- The State Partnership for Accountability, Responsiveness and Capability (SPARC) supports current government reforms and helps to improve resource management (SPARC, 2014).

Key initiatives for participatory local governance

- The 1976 Local Government Reform paved the way for a local government system in the country. It conceptualized local government as a third tier, which was also enshrined in the 1979 Constitution (Okafor and Orjinta, 2013).
- The 1999 Constitution, passed after the end of military control, recognizes local government as a third tier. However, local government remains under the control of the state government (Okafor and Orjinta, 2013).
- In 2011, Nigeria enacted the Freedom of Information Act to improve government transparency. However, access to information is often denied (Freedom House, 2014).

Challenges for participatory local governance

- Only 157 of the 774 local governments are run by elected local councils. Contrary to the 1999 Constitution, the remaining local councils are replaced by "caretaker committees", which are appointed by the state governor (Okafor and Orjinta, 2013).
- State and local governments fail to provide citizens with sufficient public services (IFPRI, 2009).
- Local elections do not occur on a regular basis (Nigerians Talk, 2013).
- There is limited transparency and accountability about the management of public resources at all levels of government. This is exacerbated by weak sanctions (World Bank, 2009).
- Women account for less than 10% of elected local government councilors (CLGF, 2013).

List of sources:
British Council, 2012: "Gender in Nigeria Report 2012."
Center for Environment, Human Rights and Development (CEHRD), 2012: www.cehrd.org.
Centre for Democracy and Development (CDD), 2014: http://cddwestafrica.org/index.php/en/.
Commonwealth Local Government Forum (CLGF), 2013: "The Local Government System in Nigeria."
Female Leadership Forum, 2012: www.flf.com.ng/home.
Freedom House, 2014: "Nigeria."
Information Nigeria, 2013: "ALGON calls for LG Autonomy."
International Food Policy Research Institute (IFPRI), 2009, Okojie, C.: "Decentralization and Public Service Delivery in Nigeria."
Ministry of Local Government, 2013: http://www.nigerstate.gov.ng/ministry-of-local-government.html.
Nigerians Talks, 2013, Amaza, M.: "Do we need local government autonomy?"
Okafor, J and I. Orjinta, 2013, Commonwealth Journal of Local Governance: "Constitutional Democracy and Caretaker Committee in Nigeria Local Government System: An Assessment."
State Partnership for Accountability, Responsiveness and Capability (SPARC), 2014: www.sparc-nigeria.com/index.php.

PAKISTAN

PLDI rank	42
Population	179,160,111
HDI rank	146/187
HDI score	0.515

Pakistan first pursued reforms for deeper decentralization in 1973 and again during 2000 and 2001. However, local governments were suspended in 2010 and municipalities were placed under provincial authority (UCLG, 2010). In 2013, the Minister for Local Government announced the introduction of a new local government law under which local government elections would be conducted, but these elections have been postponed to an uncertain date (The Express Tribune, 2014).

Local governance at a glance

- Pakistan's subnational government is composed of four provincial governments. Provinces are responsible for creating local governments with departments to administer local government matters (UCLG, 2010).
- Local governments are divided into 112 Districts (rural areas) and City Districts (large metropolitan areas), 399 tehsils (towns) and 6,125 Union Councils (UCLG, 2010).
- Pakistan has legislated gender quotas in the form of reserved seats. In each local government level and administrative body, 33% of seats are reserved for women. In Provincial Assemblies, 22% of seats are reserved for women (Quota Project, 2014).

Civil society actors

- The Citizens' Commission for Human Development (CCHD) runs education programs about local government and conducts advocacy campaigns on democratic governance (CCHD, 2012).
- The National Integrated Development Association (NIDA) supports capacity building for good governance, citizen participation, and public and private sector development (NIDA, 2012).

Capacity building institutions

- The Local Councils Association of the Punjab (LCAP) coordinates local governments in the Punjab province to promote participatory governance and facilitate joint action solutions to common issues (LCAP, 2013).

Fiscal control

- The central government holds the majority of fiscal power, though provincial governments may collect minor taxes. A substantial portion of provincial revenue is transferred to local governments, who depend solely on financing from intergovernmental transfers (UCLG, 2010).
- Local government authority over property remains suspended (UCLG, 2010).

Key initiatives for participatory local governance

- The Devolution of Power Plan passed in 2001 included electoral reform of local government structures and processes. This gave district governments authority over access to revenue and town governments authority over the functions of former municipal authorities (CJLG, 2013).
- In 2001, Pakistan introduced a major territorial readjustment that increased Town Municipal Authorities' area of responsibility and extended the levy of property taxes (UCLG, 2010).
- It was announced that the Punjab provincial government would reinstate its local government system and prepare for local elections by the end of 2013 (Daily Times, 2013).

Challenges for local participatory governance

- Institutionalizing political accountability at the local level has not been achieved. Local citizen control over civil servants remains weak (UCLG, 2010).
- The local government commission and the provincial finance commission do not have adequate capacity to protect local government rights (World Bank, 2010).
- Local governments face serious resource constraints. There is very limited access to local tax revenue and insufficient fund transfers from the provincial governments (UCLG, 2010).
- A new law and local government elections were scheduled for the end of 2013, but such were delayed indefinitely due to amendments (The Express Tribune, 2014).

List of sources:

Citizens' Commission of Human Development (CCHD), 2012: http://cchd.org.pk/CCHD_Files/Democratic_Governance.html.
Commonwealth Journal of Local Governance (CJLG), 2013:"Pakistan's Devolution of Power Plan 2001: A brief dawn for local democracy?"
Daily Times, 2013: "Features of Punjab Local Government Bill."
Local Councils Association of the Punjab (LCAP), 2013: http://lcap.org.pk/.
National Integrated Development Association (NIDA), 2012: http://www.nidapakistan.org/ta8.php.
Quota Project, 2014: "Pakistan."
The Express Tribune, 2014: "ECP postpones local government elections in Punjab."
United Cities and Local Governments (UCLG), 2010: "Local Government Finance: The Challenges of the 21st Century."
World Bank, 2010: "Procurement and Service Delivery in South Asia: Improving Outcomes through Civic Engagement, Strengthening Procurement Practices in Pakistan."

PARAGUAY

PLDI rank	23
Population	6,802,295
HDI rank	111/187
HDI score	0.676

Latin American countries are known for their high level of decentralization. However, Paraguay is one of the most centralized countries in the region due to a perceived threat to national sovereignty and its generally low density.

Local governance at a glance
- Paraguay is divided into 17 departments and 231 municipalities. Citizens directly elect their mayor. A proportional representation system is used to elect councilors (UCLG, 2008).
- The National Audit Office and the National Congress oversee local government (UCLG, 2008).
- There are gender quotas at the subnational level: "Parties are required to have internal party mechanisms to ensure that 1 in every 5 candidates in the parties and movement primaries list should be a woman" (Quota Project, 2013).

Civil society actors
- The Center for Judicial Studies (CEJ) is committed to improving the judicial system in Paraguay, increasing citizen participation and promoting effective access to justice (CEJ, 2014).
- The Center for Information and Resources for Development (CIRD) works to promote social progress and social justice by mobilizing civil society to better manage resources and share information (CIRD, 2006).
- Seeds for Democracy (Semillas) promotes citizen participation and the government's responsible exercise to improve the overall quality of democracy. They work alongside organizations and institutions responsible for developing policies and laws to ensure that laws and policies support democratic practices and initiatives (Semillas, n.d.).

Capacity building institutions
- The Paraguayan Organization of Intermunicipal Cooperation (OPACI) formed in 1971 with the purpose of promoting cooperation between municipalities and strengthening local governments (OPACI, 2014).
- The Board of Governors is a subset of the Ministry of External Relations (MER). It was created in the 1990s to act as a platform for governors to discuss local issues and future plans (MER, 2014).

Fiscal control
- Local governments' expenditures reportedly account for approximately 1.8 % of the total GDP, or 7 % of total government spending (UCLG, 2010).
- Some components of local budgets need to be approved by higher level authorities in the central or regional levels (UCLG, 2010).
- There is almost no restriction on local borrowing (UCLG, 2010).

Key initiatives for participatory local governance
- The first article of the new democratic Constitution in 1992 defined Paraguay as a 'decentralized' nation (UCLG, 2008).
- In 1991, municipalities directly elected mayors for the first time after a new electoral code was reinstated (UCLG, 2008).
- Some municipalities have been introducing participatory budgeting as a means to include citizens in financial decision making processes (UCLG, 2008).
- The World Bank acknowledges Paraguay's successes in granting free access to primary health care and basic education for all citizens (World Bank, 2013).

Challenges for participatory local governance
- The government has had trouble working with small budgets to implement successful projects and build effective public institutions (UN, 2004).
- Insufficient accountability mechanisms have been a challenge to implementing policies and projects (UN, 2004).
- Municipalities are still controlled by the central government despite their legal autonomy and the progress toward democratization since 1991 (UCLG, 2008).

List of sources:
Center for Information and Resources for Development (CIRD), 2006: http://www.cird.org.py/.
Center for Judicial Studies (CEJ), 2014: http://www.cej.org.py/index.php/cej.
Ministry of External Relations (MER), 2014: http://www.mre.gov.py/v1/Contenidos/222-autoridadesNacionales.aspx#Gobernadores.
Paraguayan Organization of Intermunicipal Cooperation (OPACI), 2014: http://www.opaci.org.py/.
Quota Project, 2013: "Paraguay."
Seeds for Democracy (Semillas), n.d.: http://www.semillas.org.py/.
United Cities and Local Governments (UCLG), 2008: "UCLG Country Profiles: Paraguay."
United Cities and Local Governments (UCLG), 2010: "Local Government Finance: The Challenges of the 21st Century."
United Nations (UN), 2004: "Paraguay: Overview of achievements and challenges promoting gender equality and women's empowerment."
World Bank, 2013: "Paraguay Overview."

PHILIPPINES

PLDI rank	16
Population	96,706,764
HDI rank	114/187
HDI score	0.654

Although the Local Government Code (LGC) of the Philippines is considered a milestone toward decentralization and governance reformation under President Aquino Jr., the Philippines is still facing different challenges on the local level.

Local governance at a glance

- The Philippines have four local government units (LGU): 80 provinces, 122 cities, 1,512 municipalities and 42,000 barangays (CenPEG, 2012).
- The Department of the Interior and Local Government is responsible for supervising the local government, and the Bureau of Local Government Finance exercises financial oversight. (UCLG, 2006).
- At all local levels there are elected government officials and local development councils for three-year terms (LGC, 1991).
- The LGC requires that women be one of three sectoral representatives that reside in every municipal, city, and provincial council (Quota Project, 2014).

Civil society actors

- The Center for People Empowerment in Governance (CenPEG) seeks to empower the marginally poor to play bigger a role in governance by conducting trainings and education on elections and citizen participation (CenPEG, 2014).
- The Galing Pook Foundation (GPF) promotes excellence in good governance, acts as a capacity building institution and awards local government programs (GPF, 2013).

Capacity building institutions

- The Local Government Academy (LGA) is paramount provider of capacity building services to LGUs. such as program designing, training implementation and forms of technical assistance (LGA, 2013).
- The Union of Local Authorities in the Philippines (ULAP) seeks to attain "genuine local autonomy for all LGUs" and ensure "efficient delivery of basic services to local communities" (ULAP, 2014).

Fiscal control

- LGUs' own revenue sources consist of property, local business and community taxes and various fees. This accounts for 32.5% of the LGU budget. Forty percent of domestic taxes (two thirds of LGU's total revenue) and 40% of income of utilization from the national wealth (natural resources) (0.35% of LGU's total revenue) are transferred as shared revenues (IMF, 2012).
- LGUs have the right to "determine their own sources of revenues, subject to guidelines and limitations the Congress may provide, consistent with the basic policy of local autonomy" (IMF, 2012).

Key initiatives for participatory

- The 1991 LGC is the key instrument of decentralization, providing "devolution, deconcentration and delegation and for decentralization of financial resources to support the devolved basic services" (UCLG, 2006).
- The Local Governance Performance Management System was created in 2001 to help measure effectiveness and efficiency of local government service delivery (UCLG, 2006).
- After the election of President Aquino Jr. in 2010, a series of reforms took place to improve governance and transparency, fight corruption, and empower and strengthen citizens' direct participation (GIFT, 2013).

Challenges for participatory governance

- Many local governments fail to provide their communities with basic resources and services (Asia Foundation, 2010).
- Corruption and cronyism pose a further problem: "local bosses often control their respective areas, limiting accountability and encouraging abuses of power" (Freedom House, 2014).
- The provisions of the 1991 LGC created vertical and horizontal imbalances whereby local governments' resource bases and tax assignments favor local governments in cities (World Bank, 2011).

List of sources:
Asia Foundation, 2010: "Local Governance in the Philippines."
Center for People Empowerment in Governance (CenPEG), 2012: "20 Years After: Revisiting the Local Government Code."
Center for People Empowerment in Governance (CenPEG), 2014: http://www.cenpeg.org.
Freedom House, 2014: "Philippines."
Galing Pook Foundation (GPF), 2013: http://www.galingpook.org.
Global Initiative for Fiscal Transparency (GIFT), 2013: "Country Report: The Philippines."
International Monetary Fund (IMF), 2012: "Philippines: Reform of the Fiscal Regimes for Mining and Petroleum."
Local Government Academy (LGA), 2013: http://www.lga.gov.ph.
Local Government Code of the Philippines (LGC), 1991.
Quota Project, 2014: "Philippines."
Union of Local Authorities in the Philippines (ULAP), 2014: http://ulap.net.ph/index.php/en.
United Cities and Local Governments (UCLG), 2006: "UCLG Country Profiles: Philippines."
World Bank, 2011: "Ripe for a Big Bang? Assessing the Political Feasibility of Legislative Reforms in the Philippines' Local Government Code."

Local Democracy in Africa: Challenges and Prospects

Mamadou Seck, Gorée Institute

The emergence of local government is centered in the practice of participatory democracy. Participatory democracy is a system, or democratic procedure, that seeks decision-making and consultation from direct citizen participation. It can consist of a variety of mechanisms, such as participatory budgeting, neighborhood councils and consultative referendums. There are three essential factors that contribute to effective participatory democracy:

• Devolution of central authority to various lower-level bodies

• The emergence, particularly in Africa, of a participatory civil society engaged with public policy

• The willingness of government authorities to be transparent about decisions

The emergence of an eager civil society has greatly contributed to the effectiveness of participatory democracy in Africa. This is being expressed through traditional channels such as elections and also by endogenous initiatives. Rwanda is a prime example of successful application of traditional participatory processes as they resolve conflict to achieve transitional justice and rectify national trauma.

Decentralization is one component of the larger process of institutionalizing participatory local democracy. In Senegal, a new Local Government Code was passed in 2014 designed to move the country towards greater decentralization and thus to more effective participatory democracy at the local level.

One example of this expanded participatory democracy is a new initiative supported by various components of Senegalese society: the National Conference. Initiated by opposition political parties, civil society organizations, employer movements and trade unions, public deliberations were held in each of the 45 departments of Senegal. Citizens were invited to analyze the situation of the department where they reside, highlight grassroots difficulties and propose possible solutions. After the National Conference, a Charter of Democratic Governance has emerged as the social project of the political opposition coalition that was involved in the process. The starting point of this policy shift was the change of the ruling party in the 2012 national elections and, to some extent, the 2009 local elections, at which most of the major local authorities, including Dakar, were won by the opposition parties that helped organized the National Conference.

Initiatives to date toward the realization of participatory democracy in Africa have been neither comprehensive nor proactive. For example, The Parliament of the Economic Community of the West African States (ECOWAS), an "offshoot" of the national parliaments in West Africa, consists of appointed members rather than directly elected by the citizens. This is in contrast to the approach of the European Parliament, whose members derive legitimacy from direct votes of citizens.

SIERRA LEONE

PLDI rank	16
Population	5,978,727
HDI rank	177/187
HDI score	0.359

Following the 2002 civil war, the 2004 Local Government Act (LGA) and the 2010 Decentralization Policy (DP) were major steps toward decentralization. However, there still remains considerable room for implementation of decentralization (World Bank, 2014).

Local governance at a glance

- Sierra Leone has 19 local councils and 149 chiefdom councils (CLGF, 2013). Each ward has Ward Development Committees (WDCs) "to facilitate grassroots participation in development planning" (DFID, 2011).
- There is a guarantee of equal representation for women in WDCs, which are elected at town meetings. Five out of ten members must be women (Quota Project, 2014).
- Mayors, or chairpersons, are elected by universal adult suffrage in local council areas. Councilors are elected on a ward basis (CLGF, 2013).
- The Ministry of Local Government and Rural Development (MLGRD) is responsible for local governance reforms and implementing decentralization (CLGF, 2013).

Civil society actors

- Network Movement for Justice and Development (NMJD) seeks to build a free, just and democratic Sierra Leone by empowering people. NMJD engages with the government about policy reform and works with grassroots communities (NMJD, n.d.).
- The Campaign for Good Governance (CGG) seeks to establish a more democratic state by increasing citizen participation in governance through advocacy, capacity building and civic education (CGG, 2014).

Capacity building institutions

- The Local Councils Association of Sierra Leone (LoCASL) maintains the partnership of the 19 member councils and links them with local government authorities globally (UCLG Africa, 2012).
- The Local Government Service Commission (LGSC) provides local councils with performance management, support and supervision for human resource management (Urban Institute, 2014).

Fiscal control

- The LGA 2004 enables both local councils and chiefdoms to raise revenue, such as local taxes, property rates, licenses, interest and dividends. Local councils and chiefdoms have to share some of these revenues (CLGF, 2013).
- Local councils' budgets are composed of transfers from the central governments and their own revenue (CLGF, 2013).

Key initiatives for participatory local governance

- The LGA 2004 provides the main legal framework for local councils and specifies 80 functions to be devolved from central to local government (CLGF, 2013).
- By 2007, Sierra Leone had a "well-regulated system of fiscal transfers from central to local government, increased investment in local services and regular production of participatory development plans" (DFID, 2011).
- In 2010, a new DP was approved to harmonize the LGA and other decentralization policies. The goal is to better empower and involve local people and communities in the development process as well as strengthen the government's collaboration with the private sector and civil society (Awareness Times, 2011).
- In 2011, a national chiefdom governance and traditional administration policy was adopted to provide a framework for good governance and, among others, minimize conflicts between local councils and chiefdoms about financial resources (Awareness Times, 2012; CLGF, 2013).

Challenges for participatory local governance

- Many Ward Development Committees face acute financial problems and are unable to hold meetings regularly. Moreover, a lack of resources and weak oversight foster corruption (CR, 2012).
- The revenue system at the local levels need to be strengthened and the revenue relationship between local councils and chiefdoms clarified (World Bank, 2014).
- The effectiveness of local councils, their accountability and responsiveness towards citizens, as well as the transparency of local councils' decision-making processes have to be improved (World Bank, 2014).

List of sources:
Awareness Times, 2011: "National Decentralisation Policy."
Awareness Times, 2012: "In Sierra Leone, New Policy to Sanitize Tribal Administrators."
Campaign for Good Governance (CGG), 2014: www.slcgg.org.
Commonwealth Local Government Forum (CLGF), 2013: "Country Profile: The local government system in Sierra Leone."
Conciliation Resources (CR), 2012: "Decentralisation and Peacebuilding in Sierra Leone."
Department for International Development (DFID), 2011, Fanthorpe, R., A. Lavali and M. Sesay: "Decentralization in Sierra Leone."
Network Movement for Justice and Development (NMJD), n.d.: www.nmjd.org/home/background.
Quota Project, 2014: "Sierra Leone."
United Cities and Local Governments of Africa (UCLG Africa), 2012: "LOCASL."
Urban Institute, 2014: www.urban.org/UploadedPDF/413101-local-government-discretion.pdf.
World Bank, 2014: Decentralization, Accountability and Local Services in Sierra Leone: Situation Analysis, Key Challenges and Opportunities for Reform."

REPUBLIC OF SUDAN

PLDI rank	48
Population	37,195,349
HDI rank	171/187
HDI score	0.414

Local governments in Sudan face major issues. The political head is appointed and given little real autonomy. There exists uncertain and unclear revenue transfers, challenging the political head to fulfill tasks.

Local governance at a glance
- Sudan is divided into 17 states (wilayat), which are further subdivided into 133 districts (Globalsecurity, 2014).
- In 2001, the Federal Government Chamber was created to coordinate relations between the state and national level governments (UNPAN, 2004).
- State governors and state councils are elected as per the Interim National Constitution of 2005. District councils, also elected, elect an executive body. Local government staff and the chief executive are appointed by the governor of the state (Abdalla, 2008).
- There is no legislated gender quotas at the subnational level in Sudan (Quota Project, 2014).

Civil society actors
- The Regional Center for Development of Civil Society (RCDCS), seeks to strengthen civil society and democracy through civic education (RCDCS, 2012).
- The Sudanese Development Initiative (SUDIA) aims to reach greater stability, development and good governance (SUDIA, 2013).

Capacity building institutions
- The Sudan Academy for Administrative Sciences trains all levels of public servants, conducts administrative research and provides consultancy service. One training focuses on decentralization and good governance (UNPAN, 2004).

Fiscal control
- The local budget of states consists of own revenues (taxes, fees, and user charges), shared revenues, consisting of 43% of VAT collection, and federal revenues (IMF, 2012).
- Local budgets have to be approved by the state (Sudan Vision, 2014).

Key initiatives for participatory local governance
- The 1971 People's Local Government Act (LGA) provides the legal framework for local governments. In 1972, the Regional Self-Government Act for the Southern Region was promulgated (UNPAN, 2004).
- In 1991, a federal system of governance was adopted which divided Sudan into nine states, and the states into provinces and local government zones. In 1994, the number of states increased to 26. However, this number decreased to 16 in 2011 when South Sudan became an independent state (UCLG Africa and Cities Alliance, 2013).
- "The process of fiscal decentralization started in 1995 when the revenue-sharing agreements between federal and state governments were declared" (IMF, 2012).
- The 2003 LGA extended the authority and responsibility of the local level, especially in the areas of health, education and development (Huraprim, n.d.).
- The 2005 Interim National Constitution instituted the decentralized nature of Sudan (Interim National Constitution, 2005).
- In 2010, elections for state governors and members of the state assemblies took place for the first time in 24 years (SCR, 2010).

Challenges for participatory local governance
- Local governments are financially challenged by uncertain and non-transparent financial transfers, and due to states' control over large amounts of local taxes (UCLG Africa and Cities Alliance, 2013; Sudan Vision, 2014).
- Local governments' lack of qualified staff and weak administrations pose a challenge to the fulfillment of tasks for delivering critical social services (UCLG Africa and Cities Alliance, 2013).
- The head of local governments is appointed and has very limited autonomy to effectively carry out mandates (Sudan Vision, 2014).
- There are few opportunities for citizens to participate in local affairs (Sudan Vision, 2014).

List of sources:
Abdalla, M., 2008: "Poverty and inequality in urban Sudan: Policies, institutions and governance."
Globalsecurity, 2014: "Sudan - Government."
Huraprim, n.d: "Republic of Sudan (North Sudan): national context."
Interim National Constitution of the Republic of Sudan, 2005.
International Monetary Fund (IMF), 2012: "Sudan: Selected Issues Paper."
Quota Project, 2014: "Sudan."
Regional Center for Development of Civil Society (RCDCS), 2012: http://71.18.75.32/en/blog/regional-centre-development-civil-society.
Security Council Report (SRC), 2010: "May 2010 Monthly Forecast. Sudan."
Sudan Vision, 2014, Kidani, A.: "Sudan Is Committed to Reducing the Burden of Poverty, IPRSP."
Sudanese Development Initiative (SUDIA), 2013: http://www.sudia.org/index.php/about-us.
United Cities and Local Governments of Africa (UCLG Africa) and Cities Alliance, 2013: "Assessing the Institutional Environment of Local Governments in Africa."
United Nations Public Administration Network (UNPAN), 2004: "Republic of the Sudan: Public Administration Country Profile."

PLDI rank	31
Population	8,008,990
HDI rank	125/187
HDI score	0.622

The Republic of Tajikistan is working on draft laws, improving main forms of local self-government and elections, and strengthening economic and financial bases for local authorities. However, decentralization in Tajikistan is hindered by rampant corruption and local leaders' inherent loyalty to the central government due to their appointment by the president (UCLG, 2008; Freedom House, 2012).

Local governance at a glance

- Tajikistan has three tiers of local government: the community level (with village and town governments), the district level, and the oblast (regional) level (UNPAN, 2004).
- Local self-government authorities, a historically ingrained governing body in Tajikistan, are elected by the citizens of a given administrative territory (UNPAN, 2004).
- There is no legislative gender quota at the subnational level (IDEA, 2010).

Civil society actors

- The Center for Civic Initiative (CCI) is an organization that focuses on establishing and promoting democratic processes (CCI, 2014).
- The Independent Center for the Protection of Human Rights aims to promote the transparent implementation of access to information via training seminars, advocacy, and a legal aid center (NED, 2013).

Capacity building institutions

- The Local Governance and Citizen Participation Project (LGCP), funded by USAID and operated by the Urban Institute, works with the national government to strengthen democratic local governance by building capacity of local officials, expanding opportunities for citizen participation, and broadening access to information (Urban Institute, 2014).

Fiscal control

- Local authorities have rights to develop and implement their own budgets and concurrently establish local fees, taxes and duties (UNPAN, 2004).
- Local budgets comprise one-third of all budget revenues (UNECE, 2001).
- The relationship between central and local budgets is determined annually. After taxes and expenditures from local budgets are forecast, Parliament establishes the local share of national tax revenues and fees, as well as the amount of targeted transfers to cover local budget deficits (UNECE, 2001).

Key initiatives for participatory local governance

- In February 1991, Tajikistan passed a law on Local Self-government and Local Finance. This initiated the establishment of local self-government and revised the administrative-territorial structure according to principles of decentralization (UNECE, 2001).
- In the mid-1990s, conventional nonprofit, charitable, and voluntary organizations came into existence in Tajikistan (UNPAN, 2004).
- Five states in Tajikistan have adopted laws regarding the activities of local bodies and local state powers: "On Local State Power" of 1994 and "On Elections of Deputies of Local Councils of People's Deputies" of 2007 (UCLG, 2008).
- In December 1994, Parliament adopted and instituted a new legal framework for local governance via the Constitutional Law on Local Public Administration and the Law on Self-government in Towns and Villages (UNECE, 2001).
- In December 1999, Parliament passed the Law on Local Council Elections, which regulated the procedures for local body elections (UNECE, 2001).

Challenges for participatory local governance

- Since the 1990's, public administration reform has essentially been nonexistent because most local governments struggle with an inflated organizational structure, outdated legislation and rampant corruption (UNPAN, 2004).
- Improvement and reform of local governments' interrelations is not carried out. This hinders necessary efforts to clearly define a framework for interrelations, delegated powers, and contract relations, and to specify the powers of local organs (UCLG, 2008).
- The national government has little time and resources to retain civil servants (UNPAN, 2004).
- Most local leaders are appointed by the president, and thus have a certain allegiance to the national government (Freedom House, 2012).

List of sources:

Center for Civic Initiative (CCI), 2014: http://tajikngo.centreict.net/en/component/k2/item/1390-oo-tsentr-grazhdanskaya-initsiativa.html.

Freedom House, 2012: "Tajikistan.'"

International Institute for Democracy and Electoral Assistance (IDEA), 2010: "Republic of Tajikistan."

National Endowment for Democracy (NED), 2013: http://www.ned.org/where-we-work/eurasia/tajikistan.

United Cities and Local Governments (UCLG), 2008: "UCLG Country Profiles: Central Asia."

United Nations Economic Commission for Europe (UNECE), 2001: "Local Government in Tajikistan."

United Nations Public Administration Network (UNPAN), 2004: "Republic of Tajikistan: Public Administration Country Profile."

Urban Institute, 2014: http://www.urban.org/center/idg/projects/europe/tajikistan_LGCP.cfm.

UGANDA

PLDI rank	32
Population	36,345,860
HDI rank	161/187
HDI score	0.456

Uganda's decentralization process has included significant shifts from appointed local councils to popularly elected leadership boards. There is evidence that the country's five-tier structure better ensures the inclusion of local citizens in decision-making processes.

Local governance at a glance

- The Ministry of Local Government is responsible for supervising decentralization and the local governance of states.
- The local government is comprised of five tiers of authority:
  - 111 district councils
  - 164 county and municipal councils
  - 958 sub-county and town councils
  - 5,238 parish councils
  - 57,364 village (rural) and ward (urban) councils
- Upper level elections are conducted under a first-past-the-post system, in which candidates run on a party ticket.
- Lower level councils are directly elected through a secret ballot (CLGF, 2011).

Civil society actors

- The Uganda National NGO Forum (UNNGOF) is a network that connects connects various organizations in Uganda concerned with policy advocacy, capacity building, policy research and NGO mobilization (UNNGOF, 2014).

Capacity building institutions

- The Uganda Local Governments Association (ULGA) hosts trainings for local government leaders to address responsibilities how to conduct business pertaining to the local council, and planning and development.
- Widespread use of the radio has strengthened transparency in decision-making and enabled citizens to participate in discussions surrounding local government and civil society issues via radio programs (JAALGS, 2012).

Fiscal control

- Grants from the central government are the primary source of revenue for local governments. The allocation process takes into consideration factors such as population, revenue per capita and area (CLGF, 2011).
- Local government also raises money through graduated tax (suspended in FY 2004-2005), market dues, licenses and fees, and - in the case of municipalities - property tax and ground rent (World Bank, 2012).

Key Initiatives for participatory local governance

- The Local Government Act of 1997 lays out a structure for local governance whereby a decentralization policy is to be unconditionally embedded (IFPRI, 2011).
- Within the past 10 years, the number of district councils has nearly doubled.
- In 2010, the Urban Authorities Association of Uganda (UAAU), the Municipal Development Partnership and the International City/County Management Association partnered to assist the government with urbanization. This empowered local governments to reinforce active community participation (ICMA, 2013).
- In 2006, Uganda's Ministry of Local Government implemented a local government program funded by the World Bank. Through friendly competition between districts, a system was created that has successfully improved participation in local governments across the country (World Bank, 2013).
- Participatory budgeting efforts have been underway, and several committees, such as the Local Government Budget Committee and the Local Government Releases and Operations Committee, were established to assist with the fiscal devolution processes.

Challenges for participatory local governance

- Uganda has faced challenges in balancing the acknowledgement of traditional leadership while bringing about decentralized government. Another challenge is that only sub-county and district level councils have political authority and the resources needed to provide public services (JAALGS, 2012).
- Local governments have limited financial resources and are thus over-dependent on grants from the central government (IFPRI, 2011).
- There are too few people qualified to effectively deliver services and carry out successful development projects. However, the central government is working to increase local governments' capacity via trainings (IFPRI, 2011).

List of sources:
UN Human Development Index, 2012: "Uganda"
CLGF, 2011, "Uganda"
Journal of African & Asian Local Government Studies (JAALGS), 2012: "Decentralization and good governance in Africa: Institutional challenges to Uganda's local governments"
World Bank, 2009 : "Local Government Discretion and Accountability: Application of a Local Governance Framework"
International Food Policy Research Institute (IFPRI), 2011: "Decentralization and rural service delivery in Uganda"
International City/Country Management Association (ICMA), 2010: "Strengthening Urban Local Governments in Uganda"
Uganda National NGO Forum, 2014: http://ngoforum.or.ug/

VIETNAM

PLDI rank	34
Population	88,772,900
HDI rank	127/187
HDI score	0.617

Over the past two decades, Vietnam has tried to largely devolve authority to its sub-national governments. However, implementation of the Grassroots Democracy Decree remains uneven and participation in local level planning is often pro forma (World Bank, 2010).

Local governance at a glance

- Vietnam has a three-tier, local government structure of provincial, district, and commune levels. There are 63 provincial units, which includes five cities. The provinces have approximately nine rural districts and 145 communes, each with 10-15 villages (IFAD, 2012).
- There is a representative organ (People's Council) and an executive organ (People's Committee) in each unit. All People's Councils are elected through direct and secret ballots (UCLG, 2008).
- The Ministry of Home Affairs has the most responsibility for local government matters (UCLG, 2008).
- There is no gender quota at the subnational level (IDEA, 2012).

Civil society actors

- The Vietnam Women's Union (VWU) protects women's rights and participates in the formation, implementation and supervision of laws and policies on gender equality (VWU, n.d.).
- The Research Center for Management and Sustainable Development (MSD) is an NGO that builds the competency of CSOs and the coalitions between the government and CSOs for the purpose of democracy policy development (MSD, 2012).

Capacity building institutions

- The Public Participation and Accountability Facilitation Fund (PARAFF) is part of a Danish funded program that supports Vietnamese NGOs through grants and capacity building for better engagement in public participation (PARAFF, 2014).
- The Association of Cities of Vietnam (ACVN) is a voluntary social organization that represents Vietnamese cities. It is the only organization of local governments in Vietnam (ACVN, 2014).

Fiscal control

- "There has been a major transfer of resources and responsibilities down from the central to sub-national level. (…) Provinces have considerable budgetary autonomy, but their reporting on expenditure back to the central level is relatively weak" (IFAD, 2012).
- In 2002, total local revenue consisted of transfers (53.6%), 100% of local taxes (24.0%), and shared taxes (22.4%). Local expenditure was 47.7% of total state expenditure (UCLG, 2008).

Key initiatives for participatory local governance

- Vietnam has had three main periods of decentralization. The first period, 1946 to 1960, began when the country's first constitution established People's Councils and Administrative Committees (IFAD, 2001).
- The second period, 1960 to 1992, focused on national consolidation and centralizing the administration (IFAD, 2001).
- The third phase began in 1996 with the development of a vibrant and equitable market economy. (IFAD, 2001).
- The Grassroots Democracy Decree (GDD) of 1998 provided a framework for the development of decentralization. GDD calls for transparency and participation, asking that local assemblies consult residents about decisions (Wescott, 2003).

Challenges for participatory local governance

- Incentives for participatory democracy are currently weak for citizens and the state. New rules and incentives are necessary to improve the quality and quantity of participation (UNDP, 2006).
- Some local authorities lack understanding and leadership skills necessary to implement grassroots democracy regulations (UCLG, 2008).

List of sources:

Association of Cities of Vietnam (ACVN), 2014: http://www.acvn.vn/
International Fund for Agricultural Development (IFAD), 2012: "Country Program Evaluation."
International Fund for Agricultural Development (IFAD), 2001: "Viet Nam: Country Portfolio Review and Evaluation."
International Institute for Democracy and Electoral Assistance (IDEA), 2012: "Viet Nam."
Public Participation and Accountability Facilitation Fund (PARAFF), 2014: http://www.paraff.org/en/about-us/who-we-are.
Research Center for Management and Sustainable Development (MSD), 2012: http://msdvietnam.org/home/.
United Cities and Local Governments (UCLG), 2008: "Socialist Republic of Vietnam."
United Nations Development Program (UNDP), 2006: "Deepening Democracy and Increasing Popular Participation in Viet Nam."
Vietnam Women's Union (VWU), n.d.: http://www.hoilhpn.org.vn/?lang=EN.
Wescott, C., 2003, International Public Management Review: "Hierarchies, Networks, and Local Government in Vietnam."
World Bank, 2010: "Vietnam Development Report 2010: Modern Institutions."

2014 Survey

The 2014 Survey is based on the same five-dimensional framework as the 2013 survey, but questions have been streamlined and made more objective. All answers are a simple Yes, No or N/A - except as noted. Each response is scored consistently: 0 for negative answers and a 1 through 3 ranking for positive answers.

Each of the five dimensions are divided into questions related to the legal framework, and people's perceptions of how well it is being implemented, giving 10 sub-indices. Each sub-index is normalized to range from 0 to 100, with 100 marking an absolute score in which all answers reflect the utmost possible positive points.

Rankings are computed in ascending order across all reporting, with 1 being best and ties being given the lower (better) rank.

1. Active Citizenry

1.1 Aware
Legal
1.1.1   There is a Right to Information (RTI) Law.
1.1.2   There is a mandatory response time for RTI requests.
1.1.3   Local governments are required to post a Citizen Charter of rights, entitlements and means of access.
Perception
1.1.4   Rank the ability of citizens to know about local government information.
(Very difficult | Somewhat difficult | Straight-forward but slow | Prompt)
1.1.5   Rank your sense of citizen awareness of their rights and entitlements.
(Not aware | A little aware | Very aware)
1.1.6   Citizens can resolve appeals to information requests at a reasonable cost of their time and resources.
1.1.7   How many days would you estimate it takes for citizens to receive responses to an access for information request?
(Less than 7 | Between 7 and 30 | More than 30)

1.2 Inclusive
Legal
1.2.1   There are mandatory public forums at the local level.
1.2.2   Public forums are required to be held at times and in places accessible to women and other marginalized groups.
1.2.3   There are quotas or reservations for women and marginalized groups in local councils.
Perception
1.2.4   Public forums are regularly held according to law.
1.2.5   What is the typical gender balance in public participation?
(Approximately 1 in 10 | 3 in 10 | 5 in 10)
1.2.6   To what extent do minority religious or ethnic groups participate?
(Rarely | Proportionate to their numbers | More than average to secure their rights| N/A)

1.3 Organized
Legal
1.3.1   Citizen organizations have legal standing in court cases (class actions suits).
Perception
1.3.2   To what degree do citizens work for their rights through CBOs, unions, associations, etc?
(Rarely | Sometimes but fearfully | Quite often)
1.3.3   Do women and marginalized groups have effective citizen groups?
(Not as much as men and majority | About the same | More so)

1.4 Participating
Legal
1.4.1   The following mechanisms exist for citizen participation: Quorums for public assemblies., Direct participation by citizen on local government subcommittees, Grievance mechanisms.
Perception
1.4.2   How would you characterize citizen participation in each of the mechanisms above:
(Poor | Active but without impact | Active and Impactful)

2. Political Decentralization

2.1 Democratic
Legal
2.1.1   The law provides for elected local councils.
2.1.2   Local elections are held regularly without the decision of higher-levels of government.
2.1.3   There are effective legal mechanisms to ensure local elections are free and fair.
2.1.4   Candidates for local office are selected by:
(Party bosses | Primary elections)
Perception
2.1.5   People vote local leaders out of office.
(Rarely | Fairly Regularly)
2.1.6   Independent (non-party) candidates stand for local elections.
(Rarely | Fairly Regularly)
2.1.7   Do the manifestos of major parties support decentralization?
(No | Some do | Most or all do)

2.2 Autonomous
Legal
2.2.1   The constitution gives specific decision-making powers to local government.
2.2.2   Who is permitted to remove elected officials?

(Only the courts | Bureaucrats)
Perception

2.2.3 In practices, the following attempt to override local decision making:
Political parties, Bureaucrats, Religious leaders, Business interests

2.3 Accountable
Legal

2.3.1 Local government expenditures must be audited.

2.3.2 Local governments must publish annual reports on projects and activities.

Perception

2.3.3 Local governments indeed publish annual reports on projects and activities
(Always | Sometimes | Rarely)

2.4 Transparent
Legal

2.4.1 Meetings of local government are open to the public.
(No | Some | Most | All)

2.4.2 It is legal to report accurate news even if it damages the reputation of a public figure.

2.4.3 The public is guaranteed an opportunity to scrutinize local policy decisions before they are implemented.

Perception

2.4.4 Local government records and data are publicly accessible.

2.4.5 Government freely allows news reports that damage the reputation of public officials.
(Always | Sometimes | Rarely)

2.4.6 Local government procurement is open and transparent.
(Always | Sometimes | Never)

2.4.7 There is a place for the community to view the local government plans (internet, local government office, library, etc.).

3. Administrative Decentralization

3.1 Decentralized
Legal

3.1.1 Front-line workers (health workers, teachers) can be hired and fired at the local level.

3.1.2 Decisions about public services can be made at the local level
(Rarely | Sometimes | Mostly)

Perception

3.1.3 Local government manages or oversees each of the following:
Primary Health, Primary Education, Water, Sanitation, Local Roads, Electricity, Police, Economic Development,

Justice/Dispute resolution
(Yes | Partially | No)

3.1.4 There are clearly distinct responsibilities among the different tiers of government.
(Yes | Partially | No)

3.2 Trained
Legal

3.2.1 Local authorities MUST receive training in the following:
Transparency, Service Delivery, Ethics, Inclusion of minority groups, Administration, Taxation, Justice/Public Safety

Perception

3.2.2 Local government is perceived as qualified to do their jobs.
(Yes | Sometimes | No)

3.3 Effective
Legal

3.3.1 Local government provides direct oversight of public services.

3.3.2 Local government receives regular data on public services (eg, enrollment numbers, health data) in their area.
(Never | In some cases | Always)

3.3.3 Local government holds public forums on the quality of public services.
(Rarely | Sometimes | Regularly)

Perception

3.3.4 The performance of URBAN local governments in each of the sectors listed in 3.1.3 is
(Good | Fair | Poor)

3.3.5 The performance of governments in each of the sectors listed in 3.1.3 is
(Good | Fair | Poor)

4. Fiscal Decentralization

4.1 Supported
Legal

4.1.1 There are objective criteria for allocating money from national to subnational government.

4.1.2 There are specific revenue streams guaranteed to local government.

4.1.3 The amount of public resources in the hands of local government is
(Below 10% | 10-20% | Over 20%)

Perception

4.1.4 Local government is perceived as:
(Sufficiently funded | Honest in managing the use of public funds)

4.1.5 Funds from the center reach local government within the

first quarter of the fiscal year.
(Always | Sometimes | Rarely or Never)

4.2 Independent
Legal
4.2.1   Local government sets its own budgets.
4.2.2   Local government must post its budget publicly.
Perception
4.2.3   Local government is effective at collecting local taxes
(Always | Sometimes | Rarely)
4.2.4   Local government is free from bureaucratic or political interference in making budget decisions.
(Always | Sometimes | Rarely)

5. Multi-Stakeholder Planning

5.1 Capacity
Legal
5.1.1   Local government has a legal mandate to produce a written multi-year plan for local services.
5.1.2   Local government has access to training or facilitation in making multi-year plans.
Perception
5.1.3   The capacity for local government to create multi-year plans is:
(Non-existent | Weak | In place but not forward-looking | Forward-looking)

5.2 Deliberative
Legal
5.2.1   There is a legal requirement to engage the public in local government planning.
5.2.2   There is a legal requirement for participatory budgeting.
Perception
5.2.3   Public engagement in local government planning is:
(Non-existent | Limited to a small number of special interests | Broadly inclusive but not forward-looking | Broadly inclusive and forward-looking)
5.2.4   Public engagement in budgeting is:
(Non-existent | Limited to a small number of special interests | Broadly inclusive but not forward-looking | Broadly inclusive and forward-looking)

Participatory Local Democracy Index

Country	Group	Active Citizenry L	P	Political L	P	Administrative L	P	Fiscal L	P	Planning L	P	Composite L	P	Avg	Rank
Azerbaijan	1	50	58	34	68	67	74	50	50	50	33	50	56	53	23
Bangladesh	2	89	55	54	67	22	48	66	37	100	55	66	53	59	13
Benin	3	60	43	54	56	80	45	66	37	100	66	72	49	61	10
Bosnia and Herzegovina	1	60	39	77	31	54	34	66	12	50	33	61	30	46	36
Brazil	5	73	50	77	37	47	25	83	25	67	29	69	33	51	28
Burkina	3	20	33	39	49	54	22	50	0	50	11	42	23	33	46
Burundi	3	80	87	93	62	87	90	83	62	100	88	89	78	83	1
Cambodia	2	80	52	54	40	67	43	62	0	100	99	73	47	60	11
Cameroon	3	30	35	51	31	33	32	83	0	0	11	39	22	31	48
Chile	5	30	30	70	43	74	29	62	37	50	22	57	32	45	37
China	2	30	42	17	27	20	75	42	47	50	33	32	45	38	44
Colombia	5	70	43	54	31	67	9	50	12	100	33	68	26	47	35
Costa Rica	5	75	52	70	39	57	34	66	44	88	28	71	39	55	21
Côte d'Ivoire	3	40	46	62	37	65	30	66	12	75	55	62	36	49	32
DRCongo	3	70	35	77	30	80	20	100	37	100	44	85	33	59	13
Ethiopia	3	100	82	93	62	94	59	83	62	100	66	94	66	80	3
Finland	6	30	95	93	74	54	95	100	62	75	44	70	74	72	4
France	6	70	52	70	43	80	52	66	78	50	44	67	54	60	11
Ghana	3	40	26	93	49	67	48	100	12	100	22	80	32	56	19
Guatemala	5	70	57	85	49	33	20	66	12	100	22	71	32	52	25
India	2	67	33	54	74	60	30	66	25	75	33	64	39	52	25
Indonesia	2	100	43	85	37	94	39	100	25	100	55	96	40	68	6
Italy	6	90	65	93	56	54	56	83	37	75	66	79	56	67	8
Jordan	4	60	66	17	49	40	29	33	12	0	11	30	34	32	47
Kyrgyzstan	1	56	32	65	41	72	42	62	51	61	32	63	40	51	28
Lebanon	4	10	61	62	37	33	11	50	37	50	22	41	34	37	45
Liberia	3	100	56	93	37	107	43	100	37	100	33	100	41	71	5
Madagascar	3	30	17	46	37	80	25	33	50	75	55	53	37	45	37
Malawi	3	50	69	93	49	80	43	66	37	75	88	73	57	65	9
Malaysia	2	10	13	43	31	47	16	66	16	25	22	38	19	29	50
Mali	3	70	61	93	80	94	23	66	37	100	55	85	51	68	6
Mauritania	4	40	36	51	25	47	11	33	12	100	44	54	26	40	42
Mauritius	2	40	52	54	37	54	36	66	37	50	22	53	37	45	37
Mexico	5	70	22	62	19	74	32	66	0	75	22	69	19	44	40
Morocco	4	80	42	54	44	67	34	83	62	75	44	72	45	59	13
Nepal	2	90	48	60	43	27	29	50	25	100	44	65	38	51	28
Niger	3	90	43	70	37	80	45	83	25	75	33	80	37	58	16

Nigeria	3	70	35	77	31	67	30		66	37	75	33	71	33	52	25
Pakistan	2	60	39	51	43	80	22		83	25	0	0	55	26	40	42
Paraguay	5	40	35	93	43	33	20		100	37	100	33	73	34	53	23
Peru	5	50	31	70	46	47	8		58	25	75	33	60	28	44	40
Philippines	2	60	52	70	37	73	36		100	25	100	33	80	37	58	16
Senegal	3	90	74	77	80	87	63		83	62	100	99	87	76	81	2
Sierra Leone	3	70	43	77	43	74	45		100	37	50	44	74	43	58	16
Sudan	4	10	78	43	13	54	27		21	25	25	11	30	31	31	48
Tajikistan	1	70	22	46	25	80	38		83	50	50	33	66	33	50	31
Uganda	3	80	13	62	31	33	34		83	12	100	44	72	27	49	32
USA	6	57	53	77	40	63	60		63	46	47	39	61	48	55	21
Venezuela	5	60	52	54	56	60	23		83	50	100	22	71	40	56	19
Vietnam	2	59	30	45	34	82	48		56	27	65	37	61	35	48	34
Zambia	3	22	6	51	34	27	4		17	12	0	22	23	15	19	51
Groups																**Gap**
Asia: C+W	1	62	42	53	43	57	38		69	26	70	39	62	38	50	24
Asia: E+S	2	59	38	56	41	68	47		65	41	53	33	60	40	50	20
Sub-Sahara	3	62	45	72	46	72	39		74	32	76	48	71	42	57	29
MENA	4	40	57	45	34	48	22		44	30	50	26	45	34	40	11
Latin America	5	60	41	71	40	55	22		70	27	84	27	68	31	50	36
Developed	6	62	66	83	53	63	66		78	56	62	48	69	58	63	11
World		59	46	65	43	62	37		69	32	71	39	65	40	52	26

Legal vs Perception

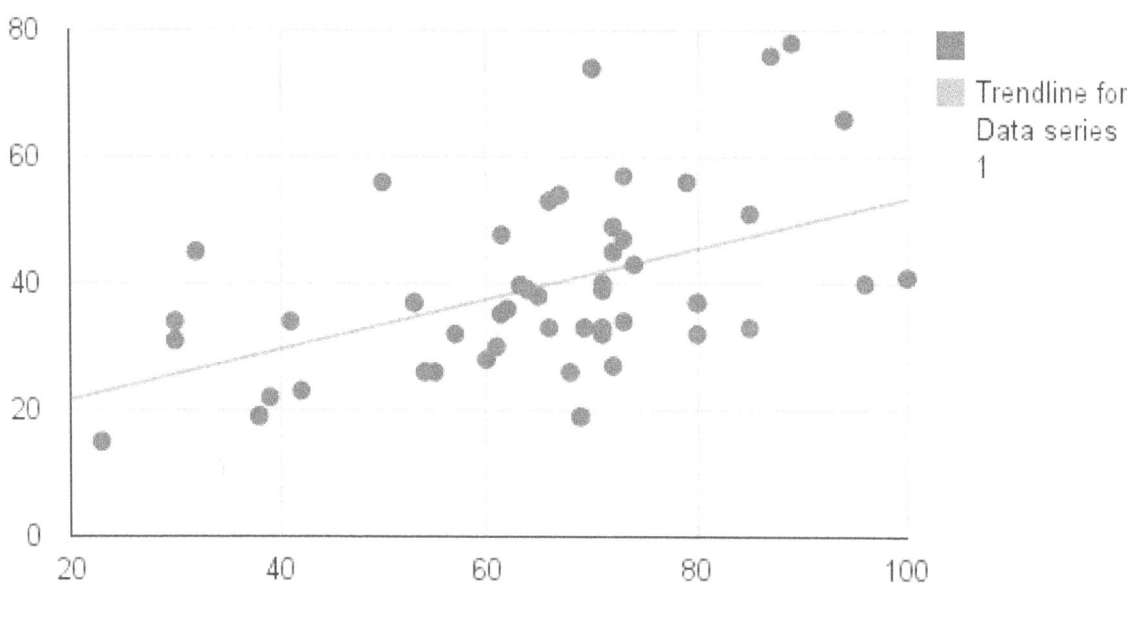

Trendline for Data series 1

PLDI - Legal